Stirring the Waters

STIRRING THE WATERS:

Writing to Find Your Spirit

Janell Moon

JOURNEY EDITIONS

BOSTON * TOKYO * SINGAPORE

This edition published in 2001 by Journey Editions, an imprint of Periplus Editions (HK) Ltd., with editorial offices at 153 Milk Street, Boston, Massachusetts, 02109.

Cover illustration by Jim Zaccaria

Library of Congress Cataloging-in-Publication Data

Moon, Janell.
  Stirring the waters : writing to find your spirit / Janell Moon.
    p.cm
  Includes bibliographical references.
  ISBN 1-58290-011-6 (pbk.)
   1. Spiritual journals--Authorship. 2. Spiritual life. 3. Devotional calendars. I. Title.

BL628.5 .M66 2001
291.4'46--dc21   00-067136

Distributed by

North America   Japan
Tuttle Publishing   Tuttle Publishing
Distribution Center   RK Building, 2nd Floor
Airport Industrial Park   2-13-10 Shimo-Meguro, Meguro-Ku
364 Innovation Drive   Tokyo 153 0064
North Clarendon, VT 05759-9436   Tel: (81) 35-437-0171
Tel: (802) 773-8930   Fax: (81) 35-437-0755
Tel: (800) 526-2778
Fax: (802) 773-6993

Asia Pacific
Berkeley Books Pte Ltd
5 Little Road #08-01
Singapore 536983
Tel: (65) 280-3320
Fax: (65) 280-6290

05 04 03 02 01   9 8 7 6 5 4 3 2 1

Printed in the United States of America

To Suzanne Schmidt, who traveled the way with me.

ACKNOWLEDGMENTS

I wish to acknowledge the caring people in my life who helped hold the vision for me as I wrote this book: Gregory Szydlowski, Wendy Schuller-Szydlowski, Jan Alice Pfau, Bonnie Marlzak, C. B. Follett, Claire Wolf Krantz, Françoise Case, Sherrill Crawford, Celeste West, Patrick Arbore, and Luke Kronenberg. I appreciate the Alanon crones group in San Francisco for helping me become my age and the Metropolitan Community Church for being there.

A special thank-you to my mother, Eileen Mains Pfau, who held me in her heart as I wrote and to the memory of my father, Emert, for believing there was something more. And heartfelt love to Lonnie Hull DuPont for being the talent that she is and believing in mine. The editorial guidance of Jan Johnson was a gift that made this happen, and thanks also go to Caroline Pincus, "the great shaper." To the wise woman on my shoulder, "Rest now, we did it."

CONTENTS

Introduction: The Hand of Promise   1

WEEK 1: THE BIG PICTURE
Awareness of Connection   11

    Day 1: Wondering   13
    Day 2: Hope Holds the Opportunity   14
    Day 3: Faith Makes It Possible   17
    Day 4: Sense of Place   19
    Day 5: Patience   21
    Day 6: Grace   24
    Day 7: Rewarding Yourself—Gift in Public Places   26

WEEK 2: THE HEART THAT EMBRACES
Acceptance   27

    Day 1: Loss   28
    Day 2: Anger   31
    Day 3: Ourselves as We Are   34
    Day 4: Differences Between Us   38
    Day 5: Life as It Is   40
    Day 6: Welcome Change   42
    Day 7: Rewarding Yourself—Spreading Roots   44

WEEK 3: TAMING THE "ROUGHS" AT THE DOOR
Letting Go of Control   45

Day 1: Releasing Others' Control Over Us   47
Day 2: Stopping the Internal Judge   48
Day 3: Interrupting the Need to Control Others   52
Day 4: Letting Go of Negativity   55
Day 5: Accepting and Reaching for Support   58
Day 6: Surrender   60
Day 7: Rewarding Yourself—Flowing with the Water   63

WEEK 4: THE FULL RIVER
Trusting Our Knowledge   65

Day 1: Receiving Knowledge Through Our Emotions   66
Day 2: Body Sensations and Intuition   68
Day 3: Releasing Overwhelm   71
Day 4: Developing Clarity   74
Day 5: Standing Up for What We Believe   76
Day 6: Finding Balance   78
Day 7: Rewarding Yourself—The Spirit Grows   80

WEEK 5: THE SELF REBORN
Sense of Self   81

Day 1: Beyond Image   82
Day 2: Changing Identification   85
Day 3: Self-esteem   87
Day 4: Boundaries   89
Day 5: Honesty   91
Day 6: Prayer   95
Day 7: Rewarding Yourself—Movement Comes   96

WEEK 6: LOVING THE MUSE THAT TAKES US HOME
Creativity   99

Day 1: Uniqueness   100
Day 2: Risk-taking   102
Day 3: Reducing Blocks   104
Day 4: Strengthening Access to Creativity   108
Day 5: Using Day and Night Dreams   112
Day 6: Commitment   114
Day 7: Rewarding Yourself—Following the Pulse   117

WEEK 7: THE PATH WITH A HEART
Integration   119

Day 1: Love   121
Day 2: Friendships and Family   123
Day 3: Work and Creativity   125
Day 4: The Body   129
Day 5: Spirituality   132
Day 6: Solitude   135
Day 7: Rewarding Yourself—Gifts Offered   138

WEEK 8: THE GREAT SIGH
Peace of Mind   139

Day 1: Forgiveness   140
Day 2: All We Can Handle   145
Day 3: Humor   146
Day 4: Gratitude   149
Day 5: Simplicity   152
Day 6: Happiness   155
Day 7: Rewarding Yourself—The Choice   158

WEEK 9: FLOWING INTO OTHER CHANNELS
Appreciating the Cycles of Life   159

Day 1: Past   161

Day 2: Present Time   163

Day 3: Transitions   165

Day 4: Aging   169

Day 5: Death   172

Day 6: Rebirth   176

Day 7: Rewarding Yourself—The Grand Adventure   179

Appendix: The Techniques Revisited   181

About the Author   187

Recommended Reading   189

INTRODUCTION: The Hand of Promise

A young mother came to me for hypnotherapy saying she wanted to develop a closer connection to her spiritual self. As I usually do, I began by asking her a few questions. To the question when in her life does she feel a presence of "something more," she said it was when she was tending her child in the middle of the night. To the question what did it feel like, she said it was a time when the outside world took on less importance and the connection between her daughter and herself felt soft and glowing. With this feeling, everything counted, she told me, her heart was open to the sky, the books in the room, people sleeping across the ocean. All she needed was a gentle reminder from me to continue using love to have more of that spirit feeling.

This book is written to help you stay close to that feeling, to be sheltered by what's true and real for you. In it, we'll use writing to develop our spiritual practice, to access that sense that we are connected to something greater than ourselves. Some call it their muse, higher power, goddess, god, the spirit. Just use whatever word or name feels right to you.

Spirituality is many things, and we each must decide what it means to us. Perhaps you feel that religion is a set of acquired opinions and not the sacred truth, and have left religion behind to embrace a more loving presence. Maybe you practice within a religious tradition but are also developing a spirituality that feels closer to your daily life. There are no hard-and-fast rules here. Only this: Spirituality is a way of living that seeks to satisfy a longing that draws us to life.

To search for our own way can be a long, slow process, but what I've found repeatedly, over many years and with my many clients and

1

students, is that writing can be your spiritual practice. It can help you become more open, develop faith to be comfortable with the unknown, and be better able to answer the question: Who am I and what am I doing here? Whatever you determine spirituality is for you, writing will help you find your way.

As a child, I used writing and creativity to save my young life from the problems in the family. I loved the bright colors of chalk murals, but even more I loved the chalk dust as it floated to the sill. I loved to paint and watch trees grow on the page under my brush. I'd write stories that felt more real than the life I lived and was sorry when they were finished. I was in love with the act of doing art. When the fort I was building was finished, I was eager to begin another.

As I got older, I realized that writing and painting gave me a sense of re-creating myself. To be creating something, to make something new, to be at the beginning of something, was to feel alive and generous and loving. I didn't yet call it a god force, because I didn't believe God was in my life. When I was five years old, our Sunday school teacher showed us a poster of Jesus surrounded by island children. Jesus was reaching out to them. We sang "Jesus Loves Us" and I remember the thought crashing through my mind that that's why God and Jesus didn't help me. They were on some island helping other little children.

And so I lived my life wanting the feeling of connection that writing and art gave me. I found I turned more and more to writing because all I needed was a pencil and paper and myself. I could write anywhere. My writing gave me a feeling of connection to my life source in an everyday, regular way. In times of despair I could write a poem, a story, or just put down what I was thinking and feeling. I learned I could ask myself questions and write the answer until I felt my heart opening to myself and others. Writing helped me connect to my soul. It is this feeling that makes me a larger person and makes happiness a part of my daily life.

In my work with clients, I often ask if they notice any connection that they may already have to a higher power. Many times a client will at first say there is nothing to build on, but then remember loving the smell of the lilies of the valley that grew in the neighbor's yard where she grew up, and wondering how that scent was made. We then explore how the smell makes her feel and what that has to do with her spirit.

What I've found is that it is often easier, and more genuine, to build on something we already have in our memory and may have forgotten than to search out something altogether new. Of course, the process of developing our inner selves and our connections to our wise powers through writing will not be a linear one. We will remember the old connections that stirred in us as children. We will remember questions we once asked. We will start to accept our feelings and to let go of our fears. And then we will find ourselves doubting those connections and feel that we're back at the beginning. We will follow our intuition to find balance and, after a good jog in the rain and a ten-hour night's sleep, the feeling of connection will return.

The exercises in this book were designed to help you more regularly find this connection, to tap into your wise self. With practice, growth sneaks up on you much like a garden when it's ready to bloom. After seeing only buds for the longest time, suddenly you are awash in blooms. How could it happen all at once? Why did it happen in just the left end of the garden this day? Was it the sun? It didn't seem stronger there. Maybe it was the soil in that section. Whatever it is, after the clearing, the seeding, and the nurturing, a pattern of growth is displayed. And sometimes, too, in the midst of the garden, are sunflowers you didn't plant. You have no idea how they got there, but they grow the fastest and tallest of all. You're glad to have them for beauty and eating and the mystery of it all. That's the way it is with writing about spirit.

The first time I taught *Writing as Spiritual Practice* as a workshop, a woman who was grieving the loss of her partner cried as she asked to read to the class what she had written. As she read, I had the feeling that doves were flying out of this grieving woman's heart. I could hear their gentle flapping wings. She told us she felt so openhearted just then and so filled with such forgiveness for herself and love for us. I knew the doves were alive in her life now and that writing had released something that had held her in darkness. Now she could move on toward her own hopeful dawn.

As you write and explore yourself, you are a part of a long history of seekers. This longing for spirituality can be traced back to the limestone caves in France where Cro-Magnon people left their ritual markings and paintings. Writing gives us the power to pull back the blankets of night and see what the light will bring. You may change. You may deepen. You may find the souls in your body and feel more connected.

I developed the process we'll use in this book out of my own feeling of overload. For years I had cast about for ways to develop my faith, and had ended up feeling overwhelmed by all the information I was getting from church, workshops, classes, and books. And so I sat down and thought about the qualities common to most spiritual and religious searches. What was it that allowed people to live with a greater feeling of soul and spirit? I identified nine key qualities: Awareness of Connection, Acceptance, Letting Go of Control, Trusting Our Knowledge, Sense of Self, Creativity, Integration, Peace of Mind, and Cycles of Life. I then intuited what each one would entail and began to sketch that out. That sketch has become the program I call *Stirring the Waters*.

Over the course of nine weeks, we'll explore each of the nine qualities in turn. For each day of a given week, you will find a discussion of one aspect or component of that quality and then several writing exercises to help you explore it further. You'll discover how that aspect of the quality appears in your life and how it can be transformed. On the seventh day of each week, you'll have a "reward" day, where you are encouraged to take yourself out into the world to write.

The first week is devoted to *Awareness of Connection*. Here we'll look at the concept that there is something more than the life we see in front of us. How we feel expansive as we sit in a redwood clearing or connected to a friend who is feeling vulnerable and tells us her fears. We'll explore how wondering about our spiritual connection leads to hope and all the opportunity hope opens, and how faith develops from our belief that connection is possible. Awareness of connection can be the insight that we are related to all other souls.

We'll use our writing to explore how our lives have shown courage and triumph. We'll remember what it is we love: where we live, the particular mosses and wetlands or neon streets and winter with the good smell of fresh rain. We'll notice how grace begins to enter our lives with a soft touch, hesitant at first, then more enduring, when we pay attention to connection.

In the second week, we begin to explore *Acceptance*—accepting ourselves and accepting others. We'll use our writing time to look at loss, anger, difference, change, and to begin to truly open our hearts to ourselves and the world.

Letting Go of Control takes *Acceptance* a step further. In this third week, we'll look at how, when we care less about what others expect of us and more about what is soulful for us, we begin to grow emotionally. Control is a big part of all this, of course. *Letting Go of Control* is saying I'm not in charge of everything. We will write about letting go of other people's expectations for us and moving into a more authentic way of being. We'll do exercises designed to help us notice how often we compare ourselves to others and how we can stop that process, and how to stop the flow of the negative and critical thoughts that stream through us. Through the process of letting go of control we become more a part of things and know that others will share our burdens. It's surrendering to life and saying "Help me."

When we reach the fourth week, *Trusting Our Knowledge* we should begin to feel a turning point in our lives. We will begin to explore the many ways in which we receive knowledge: through thinking, emotions, body sensations, and intuition. Of course, this doesn't happen all at once, but you'll begin to realize that through your writing you've been going inward for answers, and that you can recognize a body feeling, a voice, a place of truth for yourself. In this section we'll look at how to nurture your intuition so that you can have ready access to that truth.

There are many ways to let the wise voices come through. A man I know leans against a tree at the edge of the pond at San Francisco's Legion of Honor, breathes for a minute, and lets the wise voices come. A painter friend in Chicago uses Lake Michigan as her muse, finding quiet there. You, too, may discover a place in the world that can help you hear your intuition, a special place that takes you to yourself. Or you may find that simply sitting quietly in your living room helps you remember a time when you just *knew* what to do. Through the exercises in this chapter you will find ways to build on this feeling, to explore ways to release the feeling of being overwhelmed so you can hear your wise voice.

Writing itself can help. It structures your thoughts and emotions and helps you make sense of body sensations and intuition. Once we are less overwhelmed, we can find our clarity and stand up for ourselves. I saw a bumper sticker today that said, "Even if your voice shakes, stand up for yourself." The car was filled with young women laughing and talking, and I wanted to give them a power sign, a goddess, "Yes."

What can be more important than developing a bottom line that asks "Is this best for my soul?" Week five, *Sense of Self*, is devoted to this. It is designed to help you reach within so you can reach out. You'll explore through writing who you are beyond the image you project and how to deal with the changing identifications of self in your lifetime. You'll do exercises on self-esteem and developing appropriate boundaries to enable you to better connect with others.

Week six is devoted to *Creativity*. We all are innately creative, but through our writing this week we'll begin to explore how to better access our individual creativity. Creativity asks us to embrace ourselves. It is a voice in all of us that says we are one of a kind, and that even with the sun and daffodils of the world in full glorious bloom, there is room for more light and more yellow. What any one of us offers will be just a shade different from anyone else, but all is needed and wanted.

Vincent Van Gogh wore lit candles in his cap to see better when he painted at night. He took singing lessons to help his yellows "sing" on the page. We will learn to express that hunger to be ourselves. We will explore how to find pleasure in uniqueness, too. In this section I suggest that we open ourselves to the world we have within us, to our daydreams and night dreams. Daydreams draw us into the imaginative realm; night dreams give us symbolic knowledge. We will begin to decode the messages our dreams give us.

In week seven, *Integration*, we get to write about qualities of our life's longing: love, friendship, work, and creativity—issues of the physical body and how spirituality fits into integration. We will also look at how to make solitude a precious time.

The qualities of spiritual development are both cumulative and not. Sometimes, as we develop faith, we love our home more. We love the view out back and this sense of place allows us to develop patience. Our patience, in turn, invites grace to come, and we find we sit long nights on our patio writing and dreaming.

As we near the end of this process we come to *Peace of Mind*. In week eight we'll look at ways to remember that there is a divine reason for everything that happens. We are only given what we can handle. We will write about how we can foster and use forgiveness, humor, gratitude, and simplicity as part of our spiritual practice.

And finally we come to *Cycles of Life*. Chance is always with us, but so often we live in fear of what comes next. By letting go into the knowledge of cycles we can begin to act less out of fear and anxiety and more out of hope and courage. I remember a student I once had. She was in such despair about losing her job, but when she remembered the happy days of the years before, and saw that unhappiness will pass through to better times, she was able to move on. This chapter helps us connect with our spirit and trust that we can deal with what life brings. In writing about cycles, we will explore our attitudes to our past, our life's wanderings, and the present. We'll be led to consider our own aging process, death, and rebirth. Our writing will help us see the ways we are protected by our soul knowledge and our energetic spirit.

Throughout this book I'll be teaching different writing methods: *streaming* to explore your inner self and all that you might feel, *gazing into the waters* to relax and go deeper into your truth, and *dialoguing* for times of internal conflict or ambivalence. You'll use *clustering* when you want to open yourself to new possibilities and *listmake* to help organize your thoughts. I include a Buddhist *Peace Meditation*, which helps us approach writing with an open mind, and the techniques of *Dream Sourcing* and *Coming Together*, which help you make sense of your dream materials and explore what the subconscious may be trying to tell you.

Now, just a few words about developing a writing practice. We'll be using writing as spiritual practice just as some might meditate, do martial arts, or yoga—not to create works of art but to create an aware and happy self, to develop character, self-discipline, and integrity. From my experience working as a counselor and teacher, I've found that this sort of self-exploratory writing is best done if you schedule your writing time into your day.

Put aside fifteen minutes a day to start. This will be long enough for you to leave the logical world behind and allow surprises to script themselves under your hand. This time needs to be sacred. It's for your well-being and will affect everyone you come into contact with. Some of us want a room of our own to write and insist on it. Others find that a corner without a window is less distracting. The important thing is to make a quiet time and ask not to be disturbed. In time you will be able to access your wise voices easily, and that dreams and everyday happenings in life will give you answers.

When you feel ready, expand your writing time to twenty minutes, then twenty-five, and then thirty. You'll soon find a length that seems long enough to delve into the soul, a length that the spirit responds to.

On each day of this nine-week process, you'll find a few exercises to help you explore yourself in writing. If you only have fifteen minutes, choose one. If you have thirty minutes, do two. It's up to you how many you'll do. You might make a light pencil mark in your book to note any exercise to which you want to return.

Perhaps you feel that you can only write when you feel inspired. I often feel this way, too. If that's the case, then your job here is to find whatever it is that inspires you and to do it regularly, whether it's listening to the opera, walking in the rain, or reading some favorite poetry. Do whatever helps you get to the place of curiosity. This book also includes quotations and exercises designed to inspire you.

I suggest you keep a folder of ideas or images from your own life sources that are inspirational for you: walks, a church visit, an art catalog, news clippings. I have a postcard collection of images to which I am drawn. Magazines are a great source of images in ads and articles that can be clipped and used as grist for the mill.

I have a friend who comes over several times a year with her ideas and images and we share and write together. It brings us closer and gives us a better sense of community as we write during the year.

Of course, any idea a visual artist explores is thought for your journal. Claire Wolf Krantz, an artist in Chicago, explores memory and where memory goes through painting. Sculptor Bonnie Marzlak explores the sense of home. In her installation pieces, Rhoda London of San Francisco explores sayings we heard as children, such as "Who do you think you are?" and "Too big for your britches?" Katherine Westerhout uses photography to explore the mysterious world of spirit and light. All of these are wonderful themes to explore through writing.

I moved recently to a place with a pool and a large lawn. Being here, I remind myself that much of my life is filled with energy and grace. I have so many feelings and conflicts and yet I walk lightly on the earth glad to be alive. Each year gets better because I've been able to use my years to find some quiet in myself. Years and writing have brought me to this place of happiness. In my life, writing is as important as food. It is nourishment, sustenance. It can be that for you, too.

I remember the first time I fed my son cereal and how his eyes grew round as he held the solid food in his mouth and looked at me for a clue as to what to do. I swallowed and swallowed again, this time making noise in the hopes that he would follow my lead. With his eyes now closed, he took a leap of faith. Take a leap of faith with me now.

Because writing can bring us to deep and sometimes painful truths, I suggest you have support as you write, especially if you're writing about traumatic events. It's also good to have support just to keep you writing regularly. Ask a friend to join you, or start a small writing group.

Bear in mind, of course, that mine is just one way of approaching the spirit. Yours may be different. Let this structure help you get started. From here on, the sky's the limit.

Remember, we are each everything at the same time: the healing

and the healed, the doubter and the believer, the person of grace

and the person who stumbles through the storm.

My hope is that you will find more singing in your heart just by starting this process. May every bird remind you of your ability to soar, of your gentleness. May the image in your own mirror be your friend.

WEEK 1: THE BIG PICTURE

Awareness of Connection

There was a time when I was between jobs and I would wake up at night and write down my connections. I would write about my friend Suzanne, my shelter; Margie, my fun and escape; Greg, my heart; Donna, the artist of my soul. I would remember Ohio and how I loved its fields.

Reminding myself that I was connected helped me fall back to sleep. The awareness of connection makes life stable and provides continuity in our changing lives.

Today we will begin the process of developing an awareness of a connection to our spiritual force and spiritual selves. In order to do that, we must see our lives in a context of all that exists. Connection makes the tiny dot on the map of ourselves expand to a feeling that we are more than ourselves; we are souls with one another and with the forces that made these people and this place. When we connect, we join in union, an alliance or relationship, and become part of something larger than ourselves. This is the "eagle eye" that Native Americans tell us about. Writing will help us develop this big picture. By putting thoughts and feelings on paper, we can begin to sort things out and find our soul's calling.

Perhaps we remember, as a child, being aware that there was something more around the corner from our house. That's when we learned to see beyond ourselves, when we became aware that beneath the concrete there was land and mother earth. We came to the realization that truth isn't always evident and that it can be difficult to stay connected to what isn't so easily seen. You may remember trying to tell your mom that the autumn light at dusk has fairies in it.

As we get older, we often lose this sense of connection, but we don't need to wait to reestablish it. Connections can live in us whether we are in a primary intimate relationship or single, whether times are easy or hard. Look around and notice where connections are possible, right now, with the people in your life and spiritually. You may feel emotionally connected to the heart of another, such as when a friend tells you they understand and won't leave you alone with a loss. Or your mind may lead the way to a heartfelt connection. I once worked with a client who told me that kindness made her want to live. For her, kindness was connection.

Writing gives us an opportunity to explore all the ways of connection. It gives us a chance to notice the mysterious ways of God—how connection to people, art, nature, and animals can make us feel more open to our spirit. By writing about our connections, we honor them. We ask our wise selves to become alive in us.

We may hold loneliness within us, but through our writing we can learn to open the window to our own spirit and call out our name. We can find a sympathy for ourselves. We can write to make sure to include our spirit in our lives.

Sometimes you may write and nothing comes. If this happens, it might help to think of yourself as a stream meandering to the ocean, sometimes speeding over rocks in its way, other times slowed by the turn of the land or the shallowness of winter's rain. Be patient. Grace will come.

It's an unsteady and uneven trip. This is why we start this journal with the awareness of connection.

DAY 1: WONDERING

My mother was raised in a fundamentalist church where they spoke in tongues. Her gift to her children was that she didn't want the fear of God instilled in us like it had been in her. Yet she wanted us exposed to religion. My father believed in science. Occasionally, we went to a church my parents chose because it was considered intellectual rather than emotional. I enjoyed the church sanctuary, with its windows showing trees wearing their seasons, the white walls, the simple wooden cross, the vase of fresh lilies, but I put religion and God in a category for other people, not for me. The minister told stories that were too harsh. I remember thinking God was like the children on the playground who were punishing and mean.

Although I didn't connect to a church, the experience initiated in me a sense of wonder. I wanted to feel more a part of things, or part of something that would help with the sense of separation I felt with my family. Going to church helped me become aware that connection to a god force was possible. It gave me the kernel of an idea that made me wonder how it could work for me. The deep sighing of my father in the middle of every sermon let me know that this gospel wasn't written in stone. My father had lost patience with the harshness of the gospel. This sigh encouraged me to examine what was said.

Being exposed to church teachings and my father's sighs gave me permission to wonder. It had never occurred to me that you could leave a question unanswered and that that could be all right. I was used to dealing with the linear ideal of a beginning, a middle, and an end. This openness to wonder pleased me greatly.

Today we'll begin to explore what makes us wonder, what brings us to the idea of possibility, of spirit.

"When so rich a harvest is before us, why do we not gather it? All is in our hands if we use it."
—*Elizabeth Ann Seton*

"God enters by a private door into every individual."
—*Ralph Waldo Emerson*

Streaming

When writing about the inner world, about spirit, I find it useful to use a technique that I call streaming. Here's how it works: You just start writing across the page. Keep going. Write your name if you

*"I write entirely
to find out what
I'm thinking,
what I'm looking at,
what I see
and what it means.
What I want and
what I fear."*

—*Joan Didion*

don't know what else to write. Continue without much thinking. Don't stop. Make doodles to fill in the lines if you have nothing to say. Pay no attention to the inner critic questioning where this is leading. This is a time to just wonder. This is a time to be curious and explore. After several minutes of being "present" with your writing, you'll find you're in change of consciousness. In this more dreamlike state, you've really let go and are just writing. Keep going. After you've written for ten minutes, go back and underline insights and anything you'd like to continue at another time. In the exercises that follow, we'll try out this technique. You may choose between these exercises or try all three.

Exercises

1. Use streaming to explore the experiences that held the seed of wondering for you. Write about how you felt as you opened to that sense of wonder and what this search could help heal for you.

2. Use streaming to explore what you may be wondering about today. Could spirit touch you? How would this make changes in your life? Write about the good, the difficult, the unknown.

3. To whom do you feel connected? Write down their names. To what do you feel connected? Write that down, too. Where don't you feel connected? Use the technique of streaming to wonder why these connections are felt or not felt.

DAY 2: HOPE HOLDS THE OPPORTUNITY

Remember the old-fashioned tradition of putting together a hope chest for marriage? Why shouldn't we use that custom and put together a hope chest of things that help develop our awareness of connection to spirit and others: a journal, a candle, bath scents, a walking hat, a book of inspirational poetry, a book of art that lifts your spirit. Whatever helps you remember you are not alone. Whatever gives you hope.

Sometimes we know a spirit is hovering around us, but we don't take time to develop the connection. A hope chest could remind us to take the time. Hope gets us started and motivates us. Hope is a habit. The more you allow yourself time to ponder and be still, the more you become able to feel the spirit that holds hope.

Sometimes we have been hurt so badly we can't believe good things will ever happen. I knew an unemployed woman who had a great job lead but kept putting off making the phone call. Why did she do this? Why do any of us sabotage ourselves like this? Because we feel we need to save hope. We can't afford to lose it. We forget that when we're in touch with the spirit there is a replenishing of hope. We forget the saying "This, too, shall pass." If only we could see the good in the most painful times and know that there are happy days ahead.

When we're feeling that sense of hopelessness we can develop hope by writing about the good things that have happened to us. We can list our gratitudes. We can remember how it was before and how it is now. We can remember lessons learned from hard times and realize hope is there, that someone is watching out for us.

"To keep the lamp burning we have to keep putting oil in it."
—Mother Teresa

Listen! Shelter Surrounds You

You'll find me in the wind, the seed,
in the elephant's triumphant roar.
I am in the pearls of your elders,
the dirt on the far side of the moon,
the ice under the coats of Jupiter.
Naked person, listen to the hawk's cry.
Didn't you once see five hawks
careening against the dawn.
I have been humming and hammering
through the years you took to bed, in the moments
you let life fly from your hands

to live your life again, simple days
of cooking and dancing to the radio
What else is there really?
This is you. You can ride the pony
to enter your own life,
be buried in your own clothes.
Your flaws can be touched and loved.

Janell Moon

There are many ways to prepare yourself to write. One way is to be silent and let your attention focus on your body and your imagination. It's a technique I call gazing into the waters.

Gazing into the Waters

1. Take several deep breaths into your "belly." Pay attention to your breathing, in and out.

2. Focus on the top of your head and slowly shift your awareness down your body until you reach your toes.

3. Imagine yourself descending a stairway while counting from one to ten. Feel your body slowly stepping down. Imagine yourself arriving at an entryway and moving through it into a place you find calming, perhaps a quiet garden or sandy seashore. What surrounds you? Where do you sit? What do you see? Use your senses to sharpen this special place: sounds, fragrances, feelings, body sensations, something to touch, something that beckons. This is a place to use over and over until just the thought of it calms you. From this place you can explore anything.

"The very least you can do in your life is to figure out what you hope for. And the most you can do is live inside that hope."

—Barbara Kingsolver

Exercises

1. Write about your hopes for yourself, your family, and the world.

2. Using the technique *gazing into the waters*, see what might bring you hope. Do you hear birds chirping? Do you see the buds just beginning to peek through on the trees? Is the snow covering the earth like white wool? What does your special place say to your spirit? Write down your experience using the technique of *streaming*.

3. Open a drawer and take out several objects at random. Using these, write about your willingness to hope. For instance, you may take out a stamp and scissors; using *gazing into the waters* and *streaming*, write about the stamp as a symbol of sending your spirit the message that it is safe to hope for a force that cares for you. Or, you may write about why it wouldn't be safe to hope for this. The scissors may be a symbol that it is time to cut off with something, someone, or some thought. Explore what that might be.

DAY 3: FAITH MAKES IT POSSIBLE

My mom is a cloud watcher. She says clouds remind her that there is something spacious and grand beyond her understanding. She uses their comings and goings as a sign of faith: good days coming, some stormy times, some dull days. Sometimes, when she sees the clouds looking like kangaroos hopping across the sky, she knows a change is coming. She writes a prayer to her spirit each night before bed and keeps a prayer journal. She enhances her faith by just looking up to the sky.

Sometimes, after a long night's sleep, I wake up with a bounce and an enhanced faith of the spirit in my life. Or, I may enjoy the way the mustard plant makes the grass on the side of the highway glow a neon green and use this as a reminder that the spirit is all around. Always, there is a poem waiting to be written.

Faith is what is believed even without evidence. It tells us that

there is more than what we know and that good will come again.

Often it is a difficult time that leads us to faith.

Other times, something so joyous and wonderful happens that it could only be a gift from heaven. However faith comes to you, it will enrich your life.

We don't have to believe 100 percent that it is possible to live in faith; 51 percent is plenty. As Mary Jean Irions says in her book, *Yes, World,* "Faith is not being sure. It is not being sure, but betting with your last cent." It is enough to move toward the belief that you are a part of the whole.

Today we're going to write to explore our sense of faith. I find that it's useful to find symbols to help you hold faith. Seeing a morning glory might remind you of childhood wonder. Write about that. Or, perhaps you find yourself imagining an attic in a wonderful old country house, with good smells all around. You might write about how a certain smell can make you feel more spiritually connected.

Arlene, who lives in the Sonoma wine country of California, told me at dinner one Saturday night that she loved living there in August, the time of the crushing of the wine grapes. It was a "memory smell" of her grandfather, to whom she turned for comfort as a child. She has a grape leaf journal and writes what the leaves, her symbol, have to tell her each month.

"Faith hasn't got no eyes, but she' long-legged." —*Zora Neale Hurston*

What symbol might help a belief in your spirit as you allow it to bud and blossom? Listen to the wrens and write about faith.

Exercises

1. Look out your window and find the shape of faith. Write about it; explore the various shapes of meaning. For example, I see the Mexican sage plant's purple blossoms, long and thin, seeming as if they are reaching for heaven. Or, in the round pot, I feel a whole, shaping completeness in the world.

2. Try *gazing into the waters* and determine what your strongest sense seems to be: smelling, seeing, hearing, touching, kinesthetic (body sense)? Use *streaming* and write about how your strongest sense helps you with faith. The simple smell of clean sheets may trigger the feeling of life's continuity, the faith in everyday tasks. Touching a pussy willow may remind you of your little brother's soft hair and bring you back to faith in innocence.

3. Write the phrase, "Faith enriches my life" thirty times. In Buddhism, a repeated phrase like this is called a mantra. Think of this mantra as a bookmark holding your developing faith while you read this book. Use *streaming* to explore how faith can enhance your life.

DAY 4: SENSE OF PLACE

I know a poet who talks about the "gold-light fall feeling" he had as a child as the light fell slowly in the back room of the house where the family relaxed together. He'd tell his mother he had a "gold-light" feeling and his mother would give him pencil and paper. When you read his descriptions of light, moss-covered trees and the dangers of the swamps you can tell he loves the South. You can feel his connection to the heat and the southern ways. He has a strong sense of place in his poetry and his life that seem to bring him closer to his spirit.

A sense of place roots us, makes us aware of connection.

When I was a child in Ohio, I loved its rivers and gorges and roamed the land freely with my imagination. Living near the Cuyahoga

River, I was sure I could hear the Iroquois Indians in my dreams. Later, when I learned the river caught fire, I pretended it was the Iroquois reclaiming the river. I often think the woods of Ohio helped me to breathe deeper, that their wildness allowed my imagination to flourish. I remember watching the trees and writing about the spirit rustling the leaves. I would look around me and ask myself where the spirit lived that day: in the acorn, the crook of the tree, the nest? Then I'd write stories where the little girl was saved by the spirit who lived in the acorn and how the oaks protect her.

Some of us have little connection to where we grew up but still find a sense of place in nature. Perhaps you have a field near where you live that you could enjoy tramping through. A vacation may bring memories of the rain forest of Hawaii or the splendor of Yellowstone National Park. A client of mine, a man from a large urban family, often talks about the solace he found on the roof of his house. It doesn't matter where you find it; a sense of place often brings you closest to that feeling of "something more."

Today, our writing explores place.

Exercises

1. Draw a picture of the house you grew up in and of your room. Don't worry about technique. Just get the basic shapes on paper. Was there a secret place where you hid your treasures or a place you liked to play on rainy days? What about these memories makes you feel connected to your young, innocent self? Where did you sit and read? Dream? Find at least one good place if you can. Does a sense of place help you remember that you are connected to the spirit? Use *gazing into the waters* and *streaming* to explore this.

2. Use the technique of *gazing into the waters* as a warm-up, then write about a local place that you like to go to when you need to feel calm. If you don't have a place, imagine how you would like it to be. How does your body feel when you are in this place? Use

streaming to remember all of your special places and what these places did for your spirit.

Day 5: Patience

Henry Ward Beecher once said, "Anyone can bring down the fruit in season, but to labor in and out of season, under every discouragement, that requires a heroism which is transcendent."

Often, we look for quick answers, a quick fix. We don't want to do what it takes to make something happen either in the material world or in our spiritual life. Patience is what most of us have in short supply. We really do want what we want when we want it. I had one client who became terribly frustrated and impatient when he wrote about his growing awareness of spiritual connection and then about how little he lived that in his everyday life. "Never mind," I'd tell him. "The disparity is what brings us to a spiritual search." Impatience is just a symptom of our unexamined lives.

The wonderful thing is that patience is something we can learn. We can learn that the deep breath and stillness are an important part of the spiritual process, just as the spaces between jazz notes are central to music. I know of no better way of developing patience than through writing.

"Patience, and the mulberry leaf, becomes a silk gown."

—*Chinese Proverb*

In my own writing, I've had to learn to slow down and be patient. There are days when I don't have the energy. I write anyway. Write even when you have no new ideas. Ask questions: Who am I? Why am I here? Why am I tired? What can the stars tell me? How can birth and craving be quieted for a while? Our spiritual awareness often comes in baby steps. Be patient and the answers will come. Be patient with your growing sense of connection to a higher power. The serenity you'll find from your efforts will be worthwhile. Some clients say they have to pace or go for a walk or cry when they want to charge forward. They work to develop the patience to trust that a connection to a god force will come and guidance will be given.

When we are barging forward, we leave no room to hear the spirit. There is too much noise to hear the still, quiet voice. Let the quiet of patience allow you to feel your awareness of the goddess. Let hesitation show you that there is connection for you in the quiet rooms of your daydreaming.

"All fruits do not ripen in one season." —Laure Junot

A technique called *dialoguing* will help you explore questions about your life and your spirit.

Dialoguing

1. Write down the names of ten teachers in your life. These may be actual classroom teachers, neighbors, parents, or influential adults from whom you have learned valuable lessons. A teacher may also be a quality such as time or patience. Be sure to have one of your ten teachers be your own wise speaking voice, the self you are developing spiritually through your writing.

2. Now, write down a concern about your own patience. Maybe you're wondering if you should stay in a relationship even though you have greatly changed through the years and would not have chosen this person today. It could be a concern about not liking to be alone and wondering how you could learn not to feel so empty.

3. Look over your list of teachers and see which one could help you with this particular concern. Imagine a conversation with this teacher. The dialogue might go something like this:

Me: Why am I impatient?

Wise Person: You may be afraid.

Me: But, afraid of what?

Wise Person: Maybe it's that you'll get behind.

Me: I don't feel competitive. Do you think that's it?

Wise Person: Maybe it's more about fear of survival and always being busy.

Me: I want to make sure I'll do what needs to be done. It's more than that though; maybe it's a fear of . . .

I had a gym teacher in Ohio, Miss Jane Mahaffey, who knew more than anyone else I can imagine about having a healthy body. She is one of my wise teachers, a friend who knows about gentleness and taking action. I can see her with her head tilted toward me so I can hear her better. Fire is also one of my teachers. It helps me find my correct emotional involvement. Today in your journal you'll be exploring what your wise teachers have to teach you.

"Our consciousness rarely registers the beginning of growth within us any more than without us; there have been many circumstances of sap before we detect the smallest sign of the bud."

—George Eliot

Exercises

1. Use the technique of *gazing into the waters* and *streaming* to write down what you feel about patient people in your life. How could you honor the patient person in yourself? How is patience useful as you better develop your spiritual nature?

2. Pictures hold clues for what the culture wants for us and what we want for ourselves. Take several magazines and find pictures that encourage patience or discourage patience. Use *streaming* and see what you find out about the culture, yourself, and perhaps what you want for your future.

3. Set up a *dialogue* about patience between two of your teachers. Write it out and see what you can learn from it.

DAY 6: GRACE

I remember when I first heard the choir at the Metropolitan Community Church in San Francisco sing "Amazing Grace." What struck me was the word *wretch*. If someone so lowly as a wretch could be saved, maybe the wretch in me could be helped, too. I didn't need to be good or feel good, I just had to notice "how precious did that grace appear, the hour I first believed." There was something magical for me in this church, listening to the music as I sat in the pink-cushioned pews, many of the men knitting. The song continued, "tis grace that brought me safe thus far, and grace will lead me home."

"Grace fills empty spaces, but it can only enter where there is a void

to receive it, and it is grace itself which makes this void."

—*Simone Weil*

One Sunday evening Dorothy Allison offered the sermon at MCC. She spoke about her experiences writing *Bastard Out of Carolina*. She recalled her "poor white trash" origins and the grace with which the women of her family raised their children the best they could without much money, education, or class status. I could feel that the connection between the generations of women in her family helped heal her spirit.

I also noted how the minister, Jim Mitowski, encourages creative people to talk from the pulpit honoring what they had learned about their spirit through their creativity. To me, it showed that Jim is full of grace. He bows to the source of spirit. He is pleased at what greatness is brought to God's sight. He can stand aside. He doesn't need to be the voice through which God speaks. When I'm there, grace enters my body and sings with me.

Grace is my favorite word in the English language. To me, it denotes a flowing feeling of living deeply in my body. It tells me that my inside is connected to the outer world and I am traveling lightly on this planet.

With your growing awareness of connection to your spiritual self, you will notice that you are in grace from time to time and it may surprise you. It will please you, too. It feels like all is right with the world and you have stepped inside that peaceful feeling. Think of grace as a robe with which you cover yourself. It is grace's robe that flows out behind you in the breeze, a breeze that connects you to the wind and the wind to the sea and the currents and air pressure. You are connected to everything around you by wearing that robe. Grace gives us ease to find our way back to loving the world.

"I see the wise woman.
She carries a blanket
of compassion.
She wears a robe
of wisdom.
Around her throat
flutters a veil of
shifting shapes."
—Susun Weed

Exercises

1. Try asking the printed page where grace is. Look in a book of poetry for phrases to explore. Jot down those phrases to which you respond: all creatures sleep, kiss the rose of your skin, birth and craving quieted for a while. Then write what grace has to do with these random phrases.

2. Image yourself visualizing grace around someone difficult in your life. How would that help you to deal with this person? Write down a prayer for her. Write down a prayer for yourself.

3. Try to recall when you have been more generous than would be expected from your past experiences. Perhaps you did a kindness for someone who isn't always kind to you. Perhaps you were kind when you were not feeling joyful yourself. Write and explore that feeling of grace.

25

DAY 7: REWARDING YOURSELF— GIFT IN PUBLIC PLACES

We've covered a lot of ground in just one week. You may feel changes bubbling up within yourself. Sometimes just deciding to keep a journal causes a shift. Giving daily time to yourself is a great gift. Maybe you've noticed that you can sit quietly and feel a little more content. For your reward this week, take your journal to a sculpture in town and write what this sculpture has to do with your awareness of your connection to a spiritual force. (This sculpture could be a statue, a coin, a gravestone, the relief on a water or sewer cover.) How does the subject of the sculpture, what it's made of, and where it's placed reflect your spiritual development? If the sculpture in the park is an angel with a cracked base, what does the cracked base mean to you? Or, if it's a cast squirrel on someone's front lawn, how does the busyness of the squirrel reflect your spiritual development? What does your wise voice say? What can you learn from your writing today?

"To create one's own world in any of the arts takes courage."

—*Georgia O'Keeffe*

WEEK 2: THE HEART THAT EMBRACES

Acceptance

As we begin to explore the spirit, we naturally begin to look for ways to accept ourselves and others. Writing can be a wonderful aid in this process. Even just to write your name with awareness on the page is to write your name on the world. The awareness of connection that we began to develop in last week's writings begins to follow us in all our mundane tasks and all we see. We begin to notice the mud at our feet or the egret's nest high in the trees. Our hearts open and part of this opening has to do with love recklessly and wonderfully unzipping toward us.

As we become aware of connections, we begin to notice that the world gives us all of itself to accept: the mowed lawns, satin sheets, shortbread cookies, a smooth bowl to hold your tears, the rattled bone to mourn, the leaded mirror. In *The Journal of Katherine Mansfield*, Mansfield writes: "Everything in life that we really accept undergoes a change." We count on reality, change with all its good and bad manners.

Of all the spiritual qualities, I have found acceptance of myself the most difficult. As a child I had a sense of joy, and my creative activities made me feel happy, but I was expected to conform. I wasn't to have many needs. My parents valued creativity but they wanted me to fit in. These conflicting values made it hard for me to accept the exploring self that was me. I couldn't accept the self who just wanted

"Birds sing after the storm, why shouldn't people feel as free to delight in whatever remains to them?"
—Rose Kennedy

"Wisdom never kicks at the iron walls it can't bring down."
—Olive Schreiner

27

to experiment and wander, but I also couldn't give up my curiosity. I learned how to sneak in what I wanted to do, and then felt bad about myself. I would curl up with my lined tablets and write out my wishes and then write how to be good.

I hid out in my bedroom with my diary or wrote letters to a pen pal to explore my conflicts. I wrote letters to the school guidance counselor, Mrs. Ellis, but never sent them—she was for troubled kids. Already, though, writing was a tool I used to explore how to accept myself. As we view ourselves through the lens of acceptance, we begin to drift to the center of softness. We begin to forgive what went wrong with ourselves and forgive how hurt has made us act. Our writing today will be about what we need to learn in the accepting of ourselves.

"Keep a diary and someday it'll keep you."

—Mae West

Acceptance of ourselves asks us to deal with the loss of our real selves, and to say there is enough that is good. We may have lost some of joy and innocence we had as children, but we have enough to live on. Our real selves have everything: every feeling, every reaction, all of human life. We remember how relaxed and balanced our bodies once felt before hurt, and we work to gradually regain that. We are asked to recognize what is true for us, feel it, and move on, with hope and trust that all will be well. We are asked to live life as it is and value differences in others.

When we shift into self-acceptance, we live in a wise speaking way.

DAY 1: LOSS

So many times we try to avoid dealing with what is troubling us by escaping into television or addiction or just being too busy. We head home after work to eat and watch television or spend the evening with a good bottle of wine to soften the edges of our stress. We make plans for every night of the week so as not to have the time to be alone with ourselves and do the reflective work the spirit needs. We lose our wise person's counsel.

Loss is one of those things we so often try to avoid. Loss of a job, a loved one, a part of ourselves. We don't have channels for dealing with loss. But being asked to accept ourselves without dealing with our losses is like asking us to leave behind one hand, one foot, our eyes, or our shoes on the side of the road. Give up our love of writing. No more listening to stories. Sit still and learn to like it. No more laughing. There now. Just act happy and well and in spirit and everything will be fine.

But it is our human right to feel the pain of loss. It will not consume us if we acknowledge it and work toward acceptance. In *An Interrupted Life: The Diaries of Etty Hillesum*, Hillesum writes, "[S]uffering has always been with us, does it really matter what form it comes? All that matters is how we bear it and how we fit it into our lives." The way to acceptance is to understand what happened to your spirit and to be sympathetic to the pressures you were subjected to and how you gave up. With caring and coaxing through writing, you nurture and reassure the young self you once were and ask yourself to live as you once wanted, with rainbows twined in your hair. You give your wise speaking a voice. You give yourself a spirit who accepts all that you are.

Begin with acceptance of your writing. You don't need to be an expert. You don't need to be sure of your grammar. Accept how you write and think of it as a tool to find your wise voice. All that matters here is finding the wisdom you have within you.

It takes a certain fierce determination to live your life in a way that includes despairing feelings. Today we'll use our writing to begin to accept how we feel, to accept those things that are beyond our power to change, and ask the higher power for serenity in spite of all the difficulties. In *The Drama of the Gifted Child*, Alice Miller wrote about the fact that we are now the person who must notice and remember the child we once were. We must accept ourselves and yet press on for all that we can be. Writing can help us do this. You won't get stuck if you enter the well of hurt. Just remember the ladder that goes down the well also goes up.

"Although the world is very full of suffering, it is also full of the overcoming of it."
—*Helen Keller*

"Language exerts hidden power, like the moon on the tides."
—*Rita Mae Brown*

"Inside my empty bottle I was constructing a lighthouse while all the others were making ships."
—*Charles Simic*

Writing brings us closer to the waters churning within us. These waters can be stilled with the help of the soothing balm of the spirit.

Part of experiencing pain is accepting the loss that comes with being alive. With loss, we may feel a sense of protest that includes feelings of disbelief, denial, shock, anger, and self-criticism. We may experience changes in our sleep, appetite, and digestion. We may cry and experience forgetfulness. Then we may feel despair and agitation and want to withdraw socially. Next we may detach from our feelings and feel apathy. We may find ourselves acting in a "zombielike" way and feel that nothing has much meaning. We may feel all of this at the same time.

Writing helps us become new in the awareness of ourselves. There is a wise force within you waiting to speak. Let it.

Exercises

1. Use *streaming* to explore what your well of loss might hold. How deep is it? How wide? What would happen to exploring past feelings of loss if you lowered a ladder into the well so that you could go down into the well and climb out whenever you wanted? What experiences of loss do you need to explore?

2. Use *gazing into the waters* and then the technique of *dialoguing* with a teacher about loss in your life. Acceptance is saying yes to what the day brings. Write down what loss needs more work so that you could live this way.

3. Although you would never choose pain, write about the gifts of those hard times. Write what you know about going into your feelings and then becoming more than the feelings. Find out where the hurt settled in your body by just sitting quietly for a while and noticing where the hurt and anger seem to be residing. Does it need understanding, soothing, a promise from you? Speak to and for that part. Look for any lessons that may be hidden in the pain.

Use these random phrases to do *streaming* on the losses in your life. Then write down random phrases from a book you have and do more *streaming* on losses. Examples of the phrases are: rebirth of tall trees, anything can be moved, horses move through me, mirrors and dreams and moving things.

4. Write about the dark. Write about the light. Write about the changing of the night to dawn and what you see.

DAY 2: ANGER

Often, one of the hardest things to accept in ourselves is anger. It's not considered a "nice" feeling, and we often want to pretend it's not there. After all, we don't want to be seen as an "angry person," do we? A little mad, perhaps, but not angry. Instead, we justify our behavior ("I had a good *reason* for that outburst!") when what we really should do is accept the fact that we are angry and that we have a lot to be angry about! Okay. That's a fact. Where our wise person enters is in how we deal with that fact.

One of my clients is able to express anger with true kindness in her voice. It's amazing how easy it is to listen to her anger. Her words are clear. She holds no threat of retaliation or violence in her words or tone. She speaks to express herself and not to defend herself. She tells her boyfriend she doesn't want to go camping because it's too much work. Yes, the sky was heavenly and the sound of the crickets comforting, but, for her, it was too much nature and not enough soap and water. And she didn't like all the setting and packing up. She doesn't say she is right or that she is justified in her feelings. She doesn't demand he change. The request to go camping again is not an affront to her ego nor does it need be to him. She has an opinion and she feels strongly enough about it to express it. She feels good about herself in doing so and accepts that some things make her mad, even in memory.

When you feel righteous anger you can ask yourself: How can I feel my anger, and what can I do and how can I change the situation?

"Anger stirs and wakes in her; it opens its mouth, and like a hot-mouthed puppy, laps up the dredges of her shame.

Anger is better.

There is a sense of being in anger.

A reality and presence.

An awareness of worth."

—*Toni Morrison*

31

Do I have to accept that this is out of my hands and feel the anger and go on? Am I mature enough to know that in some situations I lose and some I can affect? Do I choose my battles well?

Say your girlfriend read your journal without permission. You might well get mad. You might tell her the journal is private and you feel violated. You can tell her how much it would mean to you if you could have a private place for feelings you are working through. What's important is that you take care of your resentment and your spirit. *Streaming* (see appendix, pg. 181) is a great technique for exploring the feelings that are triggered by someone reading your private thoughts. You can then share these explored thoughts with your friend so she knows your feelings. This is using anger for intimacy, not to hurt someone.

I have one friend who has learned to speak up when she's angry with me. Because she cares about me, she says, she wants me to know how she is feeling. Sometimes I wish she wouldn't! Once she told me she was upset because I was in a new relationship and spending less time with her. She asked me to reexamine my priorities. My response, of course, was up to me.

She taught me that anger is appropriate when it is expressed in a compassionate way. She reminded me that anger is the place in us that says no. It is a warning sign that something is going too far. She confided in me that she writes out what she will tell me so she doesn't blame me. I think to myself that it must not be so easy for her to express anger compassionately without practice either.

Compassionate anger is an expression of feelings. It informs and communicates. It desires a response but does not insist on one. It *never* includes violence. Once we express compassionate anger, we let the outcome go and feel satisfied in the expression of the feeling.

In accepting your anger you need to understand that anger is not a waste of time; it is carrying a message for you. "Anger is a signal worth listening to," says Harriet Lerner, in *The Dance of Anger*. There'll be no flooded world left behind compassionate anger. You'll be a person others can trust because you'll be telling the truth. A feeling, anger, was triggered in you and that's fine.

When we repress anger, we sometimes experience anxiety, jealousy, self-pity, resentment, stress, physical discomfort, and depression. Needless to say, these feelings don't allow us to rest as the moon circles the night sky. The restful place inside of us is painted with conflict. Unreleased anger can take up too large a place in our feelings and body. Think of people who seem crusty. We know enough to be careful of them because we sense the hidden whip of their anger. If we stop and consider their lives, we know that they would be better served if they would acknowledge that their rain barrel of anger is overflowing.

"Through anger, the truth looks simple."

—Jane McCabe

Accepting the fact that others may get mad at you is a sound step to intimacy. We have every reason to believe, just as the sun sets in the west, that the time will come when we will trigger anger in our dearest friends. A student in a community college class on anger once said that she trusted her friends only after their first fight. It wasn't until then that she knew whether she would be treated well or mistreated. Her wise voice wanted to see a whole person and then determine who could be trusted.

Through our writing/spiritual practice, we are learning to accept ourselves as human beings even when there are times when our anger feels like seawalls bursting in the pounding tide.

It's hard to get to a place of compassionate anger, but writing can be an enormous help. You can lift yourself from a situation of despair by reminding yourself that anger will pass and you will dance again. Let the midnight garden glow under the moon's light and appreciate darkness for what it offers. Enjoy the morning; welcome the noon. We promise ourselves to be angry in a way that we can accept and practice, practice, practice.

Exercises

1. Write down the times in your life when you felt and expressed anger. Was it compassionate or closer to rage? Explore how knowing the difference might have helped you accept the voicing of anger. Would the anger have been easier to accept if you had expressed it differently?

   Use *streaming* to explore how your anger is "the shape of your family's eye." Another way of saying this is: How did your original family express anger? Now compare this to the way you express anger. How are you the same? Different? Are you reacting to someone's anger or choosing how to deal with your anger for yourself?

2. Name three things you are currently angry about. Can you change the situation? Yourself? Or is this a matter of acceptance? Can you think of some ways to release your anger without hurting yourself or others? Write about that.

DAY 3: OURSELVES AS WE ARE

"The fabled musk deer searches the world over for the source of the scent which comes from itself."

—*Ramakrishna*

Acceptance is like saying yes to something to which we usually say no. Today we'll begin practicing saying yes to ourselves as a person with behaviors we both like and dislike, and no to the patterns that take us away from our natural self. We'll begin to recognize an important distinction: We can love ourselves and not our patterns. If we want the spirit to become more alive in our lives, we must do the hard work of accepting ourselves.

Many of my clients come to me feeling as if they have problems, but their families are pretty healthy. Their problems, they say, are "just them." Others feel anxious but think they're the only one who has managed to break free from their family's dysfunction. Neither is true. We are a part of the family we were raised in. We can't help but be affected by them. Accepting that truth is part of our growth path.

Writing your life story can bring you to better acceptance of your history and yourself. This can be done in fragments or as autobiography.

Autobiographical vignettes can help you better understand yourself and how you were affected by your family.

A student of mine moved around a lot as a child, so now she likes to stay in one place. She wants her family around and tells me she only really relaxes when they are all home together. She brings to her marriage a sense of anxiety and doesn't like it when her husband travels for his job. She says he is compassionate but that he finds her fear draining. Her children have developed fears of their own. The youngest, however, seems to be a daredevil, requiring a lot of the family's attention.

This woman found that writing vignettes about growing up helped her anxiety. The thought of each apartment would jog her memory. She wrote of her fears and how she both hid and faced them. Writing helped her see how resilient she was. She realized she did very well at facing a lot of change and saw her resiliency as a strength she hadn't recognized before. She wrote out her courage and now reminds herself that fear is one feeling among many that she holds in her body's memory. Writing helps her accept what is happening in present time without triggering the past.

"Writing a journal means that facing your ocean you are afraid to swim across it, so you attempt to drink it drop by drop."
—George Sand

Many of us carry the sounds of the nights when we were cold

and not cared for. In fear and anger, everything is caught; even

the soul's attention. We must write to the wise person within us

and ask for help.

As Buddha said, "We are the lamp." We are the source for our own light. No one can restrict us or make us feel a certain way, not for long anyway. We are either open to our spirit or we aren't.

Clustering is a technique to use when we're not sure what is triggering our feelings. It opens us to new possibilities. Sometimes we feel that something is holding us back and we can't put our finger on the source of the discomfort but we sense it's from our past. Clustering is useful because the free association method of the technique helps open the doors to our subconscious. Clustering may give you clues as to why your hatchet is swinging today. You may see what you are doing today in a different way and this insight may change your mood or actions. Here are the instructions for Clustering. We'll be using it in the exercises that follow.

Clustering

Begin by choosing a word you want to write about. Write it in the center of the page, then write down every word that comes to mind even if they don't make sense. Write down words that seem out of place or silly. You can work in a circular fashion. Keep concentrating on doing this and you'll feel a change in your consciousness and words will just occur to you. Write them down quickly before the judge within censors them. Start with the word *muse* and write three words that *muse* brings to mind, such as *writing, music,* and *nature.* Write down an association for each of those words as they appear. Below is an example of a completed cluster.

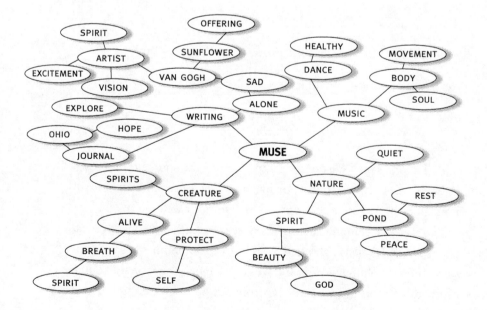

Notice how one word leads to another. Sometimes your mind will jump to a more concrete word or one that is most unexpected. Do the clustering in whatever way works for you and you'll seed your fertile soil. Start with the word *muse* and see where it takes you. Later you can do some streaming from the ideas or feelings that emerge from the cluster. You can take a "wing" of the cluster and do some *streaming* on that section and see what new insights arise.

Exercises

1. Remember a recent situation in which you didn't like the way you reacted. What feeling was evoked by that situation? Sadness? Anger? Use the main feeling as the center of a cluster. *Cluster* for five minutes. Look at what you've written and select one word or section of the clustering and explore it further with the method of *streaming*; write for ten more minutes. Underline anything you'd like to return to later. Underline any insights. How does this exploration help you accept your feelings?

2. Look out your window and find two unrelated objects. Write what these two objects have to do with accepting yourself so you can better feel your spirit. *Cluster* for two minutes. Use *streaming* for five minutes. What did you find out about yourself? For instance, say you saw a fence and a chair. The fence may be about the way you hold yourself back, how "fenced in" you feel.

   The chair could be the place for judgment, to have a time out and to sit so you can better develop spiritually.

3. Write about a miracle of acceptance that you would wish in your life.

DAY 4: DIFFERENCES BETWEEN US

It's quite a job to accept ourselves as we are. A lot of us get hung up thinking that acceptance means agreement. But to truly accept means to look upon different people with kind regard, whether we agree with them or not. Accepting the diversity within the human family means letting others be. When we do this, we can stop pushing the river and relax.

"The fact that we are human beings is infinitely more important than all the peculiarities that distinguish human beings from one another."
—*Simone de Beauvoir*

How can we be generous in spirit to those different from us? Sometimes it's hardest to accept differences in the ones we love the most. We have been taught that we are safe when others agree with us and confirm our reality. In *You Just Don't Understand*, Deborah Tannen talks of how "the ground on which we stand seems to tremble and our footing suddenly unsure" when those closest to us respond differently from us. We can explore in writing and ask our spirit to help us not feel threatened. We can ask what our fearful feelings are about and how they can be released. Were you hit when you differed from your family? Shamed? What feelings come up now when someone opposes your view?

As we go along our spiritual path, we no longer want to automatically erase people from our lives because they say or do something that hurts us. We need to accept other people's actions, and our own involvement with them, with more compassion.

"We must learn to regard people less in the light of what they do or omit to do, and more in the light of what they suffer."
—*Dietrich Bonhoeffer*

As we learn the skills of speaking up and talking things through, our acceptance of the strengths and weaknesses of others grows because we can be honest and clear the air. We can learn to live beyond black and white, total rejection or total approval.

In the past, Mara would have ended her friendship with Tim, her ex-boyfriend, because she was angry when he tried to date a friend of hers after their intimate relationship was over. Instead, she told him it felt too close for comfort and that she didn't like it. With writing and prayer, she better understood how much she had hurt him when she ended their relationship. Writing helped her look at the whole picture and better accept that she and Tim had been going through the difficult process of breaking up, trying to be friends, and now regrouping in new partnerships. She needed to be kinder to him and accept that they would find their way with their friendship intact. She might not have felt comfortable with what he did, but she needed to hang in. She needed to ask her wise speaking voice how to be honest yet generous.

It is easier to accept differences if we become aware of the messages within us. These messages—possibly things said about other races or foreigners—may have been said to us or around us when we were children. The more we explore these internalized messages from our past, the easier it is to reject or accept them, and live according to chosen or newly thought-out values. Values that are sorted out are easier to live by even when challenged. It is when we feel conflicted that it is difficult to live in a world whose values are different from ours.

"Poor human nature, what crimes have been committed in thy name!"

—*Emma Goldman*

Once you have come to terms with the various voices within, you can choose your values without so much anxiety over what others are doing. You can be joyful and happy even when your values are not those of the majority.

Exercises

1. Write on what the authority figures of your childhood had to say about making lots of money, about spirituality and religion, about taking it easy between tasks. Write on whatever makes you feel different from the group and determine how that affects the way you feel about yourself. You may not believe in these values even if you have deeply internalized them. Make yourself current by writing. It's important to know what you now value and what that does to your self-image if judged by the new valuing.

2. Use *streaming* to write out how you deal with people who have values different from yours. Give the details. Reveal a secret. How can you move toward the unknown?

3. Choose an image that repels you and write about it. How can this be related to your shadow life? Your spirit life? How does this tie into accepting differences in yourself and others. Use the technique of *gazing into the waters* and then do *streaming*.

DAY 5: LIFE AS IT IS

I am sometimes asked if accepting one's life makes us too passive. The message of acceptance can remind some people of the religious message to serve the church and accept our humble lot.

I think acceptance is more active than that. Accepting your life gives you a sense of peace in what you have been able to create for youself and what you've been given. Why not see the good in all that surrounds you and accept the difficulties for the lessons and wisdom they bring? This acceptance will make your days more serene. Why not give any change you want a time to mature and accept this day?

We tend to think in either/or ways. We haven't learned much about holding two seemingly contradictory thoughts at the same time. We must come to accept that our mother was a good mother and a bad mother all at the same time. Or that a job can be both satisfying and not satisfying. We need to accept the good that the day brings and at the same time work for whatever change we want.

"The problem is not that there are problems. The problem is expecting otherwise and thinking that having problems is a problem."

—*Theodore Rubin*

I remember listening to an ex-priest, now a writer, tell of being near starvation during the war in Poland. A German soldier threw him a potato behind the backs of his comrades and gave him the sign of the cross. Could he have known the prisoner was a religious man? Would it have mattered?

The ex-priest said that after this incident he expected kindness to pound ahead on any hard hill. His life has been one of giving and receiving good deeds. He writes what he is grateful for each morning. He'll tell you that the door to his soul was the potato and the pen. He's content with the days he's offered.

Should you take a risk and leave a job, a relationship, a city, or even a way of life? You can write and ask for guidance, ask the wise speaking force to be with you as you work through your concern. Rest in the knowledge that wherever you go, you are taking yourself, and so question and explore.

With writing, we bring life in deeper, like a deeper breath, and shift though our experiences. The sense of sacredness of words, which the poet Rainer Maria Rilke named "the deeps into which your life takes rise," can be ours.

"I learned that you should feel when writing, not like Lord Byron on a mountain top, but like a child stringing beads in kindergarten— happy, absorbed and quietly putting one bead on after another."

—Brenda Ueland

I often remind clients that spiritual work is a form of action. Therapy, reflective work, and writing are actions. Oftentimes the first appropriate step toward dealing with a concern is to ask your spirit what you need. Writing helps clarify conflicting ideas and helps us to understand the different parts of the concern. Write to reach better acceptance of your life by thanking the creator for what you have.

"All life is pattern . . . but we can't always see the patterns when we're part of it."

—Belva Plain

One good route to accepting life is to do reflective writing on acceptance. *Listmake* is a good technique for this.

Listmake

Listmake organizes your thoughts and can be used as a jumpstart for streaming. To listmake, make a list of what you like about yourself. Make a list of what feelings you'd have to give up if you were to live as if you really liked these things about yourself. Now use streaming and imagine yourself in a situation where you really liked yourself.

Exercises

1. *Listmake* all you can easily accept in your life: the garden, the changes of weather, your child, your friend. *Listmake* the challenges you're facing today. Make a third list of how the things on your

easily acceptable list can help with the items on your list of challenges. Use the technique of *streaming* and explore how what is strong and good in your life and attitude can help with your challenges.

2. Leaf through a magazine and cut out the pictures to which you are drawn. Art and pictures of all kinds hold clues for us to learn about our spiritual life. We respond to one image and not another because of who we are. Compile a list of what attracts you to each picture. From this list do the technique of *streaming*.

DAY 6: WELCOME CHANGE

"A person can run for years but sooner or later he has to take a stand in the place which, for better or worse, he calls home, [and] do what he can to change things there."

—Paule Marshall

"Change is the constant, the signal for rebirth, the egg of the phoenix," as Christina Baldwin said in her poem "One to One." Change is what we can rely on. Change can make the future seem like an adventure. We can use our writing to shift our attention from a fear of the life scattering at our feet to a wondering over the lanterns about to be lit on our journey.

I remember reading of a conference where a group of famous crones gathered to discuss wisdom and aging. Great names were in attendance; women of art, spirituality, psychology, politics, and business. They came up with several circumstances and qualities they had in common. First, they all had had hard times. Second, they survived. Third, they survived with humor intact and a contentment of the day. Fourth, they retained a curiosity about coming times of silk and fires.

"Would that life were like the shadow cast by a wall or a tree, but it is like the shadow of a bird in flight."

—Talmud

It would be a tragedy to never change. It is a waste of spirit to grasp on to what we have and try to allow no change. We change even when the hard-crusted hill of ourselves looks the same. It is the sand in the years of our lives that shift us; we grow wiser or meaner. Change is growth. Age gives you a chance to be happy with change and be a happy person. Sometimes you have to make a fuss and make change happen. Sometimes change will come to you on its own. Like a train, change can come barreling down the track, and sometimes it changes both what we wanted to hold on to and what we wanted to be rid of. We need to welcome change and know that the spirit will help us cope with what is offered.

By using writing as your spiritual practice you can question your fear of change. A client opens her kitchen junk drawer when she feels stuck and pulls out the first three things she sees. She writes using these items as a metaphor for change in her life. For instance, a small golf pencil reminded her of the trail among the green hills beyond her housing project where she used to walk and watch the sunset. Walking was available to her and calmed her in times of transition. A recipe for avocado chicken was a metaphor for having friends over and staying close when she was uncertain of her future plans. A paper clip reminded her to stay in close touch with loved ones.

"I shall live badly if I do not write, and I shall write badly if I do not live."
—Françoise Sagan

I wrote a poem that in part says:

> The dried roses are on the shelf,
> the lilies strewn across time asking
> me to change, come to change,
> and reality.

I believe we are asked to come to change and reality. I think we can learn to handle well whatever comes.

Exercises

1. Write about a time when change happened faster than what you were ready for. How did it feel? Remember another time when you

were on a pleasant plateau, your life stable and happy, and change came. What do you know about change? Welcoming change?

2. What if change were the norm and status quo the exception? What would mothers teach their kids? Use *streaming* to explore this.

3. Write about how you can best help change begin in friendship, work, creativity, and your health.

DAY 7: REWARDING YOURSELF— SPREADING ROOTS

*"Trees were
God's first temples."*
—*William Cullen Bryant*

Notice any changes that have happened, no matter how small. Are you feeling more accepting of yourself? Today, as your reward, I'd like you to find a tree that you can use as your favorite tree. I've had many in my life: the weeping willow in my backyard, a pepper tree with a bench in front of it in Golden Gate Park. Now I love the maple that grows not far from the shore of the bay with a picnic table nearby. A tree is a wonderful place to take a journal and ask how to let go and find acceptance. Find a tree near you and ask your spirit why you like this tree. What can it promise you? Then use *streaming* to explore how accepting you can be of this place, this day.

WEEK 3: TAMING THE "ROUGHS" AT THE DOOR

$\mathcal{Cee}$ Letting Go of Control

How much control over our lives do we really have? How much do we need? Our houses may be spotless, our desks organized, our pennies rolled in penny rollers, the bills in our wallet sorted from $1 to $20. Even with all this, life will keep on rolling and our hair may blow wildly or our papers will fly out the window in the afternoon wind. To see the truth of this, notice the ways that just when everything is going fine at work, things in your personal life fall apart. Or think of the times when you stayed in tight control of a relationship; what happened to you, your partner, and the relationship?

We have learned that control makes us feel safe especially if we come from a family that seemed in chaos. Yet the time comes when we must be finished with yesterday. By focusing on what we must do and letting the results take care of themselves, we let go. By paying attention to our feelings, our honesty, and letting the words across the page come to a conclusion, we let go. By not knowing what will happen but doing things with good intentions, we let go. And what a relief it is!

It's human nature to want what we want when we want it. And how hard it is to stop. Our writing can help us see what this immediacy is all about. What's the rush? Why not open our hands and let life come find us for a while.

"We are most deeply asleep at the switch when we fancy we control any switches at all."
—Annie Dillard

I once read that Van Gogh had felt he was trying to control life by trying too hard and wrote to his brother, Theo, "Maybe I'm tired because I've walked a long way."

Control is engrained in every aspect of our lives. How we use control affects our relationships with family, friends, and intimate partners. Streaming, clustering, listmaking, and dialoguing are all wonderful tools for helping us find our way out of the tight knots. But how can we deal with family patterns that we don't like if we don't control the yelling or the smoking? How can we act more positively around our family if we don't exert control? How can we set better boundaries without controlling? What is an equal relationship? We don't need to know the answers, but our writing can help us question and explore. Surprisingly, insights may come simply by formulating questions.

As we let go of control, we learn to embrace our own imperfections, to work out a pact with ourselves to let ourselves be. "Let me be in the hand of the great mother," we can say, and with this awareness, we are.

In this process of letting go of control, we will also see how we control others. "People who make some other person their job are dangerous," says Dorothy L. Sayers, in *Gaudy Night*. When we focus on another person we can't help but control them. We'll have an opinion of what they should or shouldn't do and we need to say it. And we'll resent them if they don't take our advice. Or we ignore the hardships we bring to ourselves and others. Say, for example, in your attempt to control your daughter, you make it known that you will be angry if she doesn't come home for the holidays. Rather than ask what she and her family want to do, you insist. She may come, but she will be full of resentment and it will harm your relationship in the long run. No matter how well-meaning we may be, we are interfering with the right of others to find out for themselves or to make their own choices. Even if they are less able, it is still their life. We all have our own path, our own wise speaking person.

To allow the fragrant river of life to flow through us, we must let go of perfection and our negative thoughts. This means letting go of the control our internal judge has over us, the shoulds and oughts. This week our writing exercises will explore lessening the power of those difficult experiences that make us feel defeated.

DAY 1: RELEASING OTHERS' CONTROL OVER US

When we are young, we adhere to the messages of authority. We internalize the voices that say this is right, this is wrong. This is good behavior, this is bad. I remember my grandmother cautioning me not to be too full of myself. She couldn't understand that I was excited and that even the sky seemed cramped, blazing its purity. I wanted to climb the oak to the moon. I wanted to write in the woods and share my stories. I wanted to wake with morning playing with me as it peeked through my wooden shutters. I couldn't lumber out of bed and dress without first racing to the window to see the day. Grandma didn't understand that trying to control my high spirits would not keep me safe but rather would hurt me. It took me many years to change the feeling of control she had over me because I didn't want to feel as if I were bad.

"I was always looking outside of myself for strength and confidence, but it comes from within."

—Anna Freud

We have a choice not to follow the scripts of our families. The internalized voice of your father may make it difficult for you to be introspective and searching. His voice may tell you to be practical and get going. Yet reflective work may be the most practical way for you to live in spirit and find the work that's right for you.

There's room for all of us, even if we don't fit the pictures on television or in the magazines. We don't have to be controlled by what other people expect of us, but it can take time to be free. It's a process. Each time you take a step in the right direction, write about it. Affirm it. Write down what you would like to be like. To look like. What values you want alive in your work. Then work on becoming that person.

"The curious paradox is that when I accept myself just as I am, then I can change."

—Carl Rogers

Exercises

1. Write down a present concern. Think of what your mother would say. Your father. The church you were brought up in. Your siblings. Whose "shoulds" are affecting you? Now do *dialoguing* with that person and see what is positive in what he or she is saying? Now dialogue with a chosen wise speaking teacher and see what you can learn.

2. Write down the messages to which you don't want to respond and instead put down what you want for yourself. Write whatever comes to mind when you think about trusting that everything will work out if you follow yourself. Write down the things you're not sure of and use *gazing into the waters* and *streaming* to explore these uncertain actions.

3. Using *streaming*, write what happens when you try to control someone. What are you trying to achieve? What would happen if you didn't control the outcome? What would you have to do then? How could you do that?

4. Cut up a page from a newspaper and put the pieces in a bowl. Lift out the fragments or lines and write, using the streaming technique. By using this random kind of writing we can change the frames of meanings we have with control. See what you come up with.

DAY 2: STOPPING THE INTERNAL JUDGE

As we let go of control, up pops perfectionism. So often we accept imperfections in others but are hard taskmasters with ourselves. Most of us have a difficult time letting go of control and realizing that we are human and imperfect. We can't always do things just right. If we had to do things perfectly each time we set out to do a task, we'd never try anything new or challenge ourselves. We'd never write a book or ride a bike.

I love thinking that god loves the crawling child in Jesus. We need to love the crawling child in ourselves. After all, if the goddess wanted us to be perfect, wouldn't we have been born as adults who know all the answers and not gurgling children unable to say much more than goo?

We are making our way imperfectly. We are looking for progress not perfection. No one but you knows where you started and how far you've come. Your journey needs to be your only measure.

Think of the last time you compared yourself to someone and found yourself better or worse. Comparison is a mirror that finds your life wanting. It is a variation of looking for perfection. Part of letting go of control is being kind to the part within us that judges and compares. Remember the goddess is with you. Wherever you are, you are on sacred ground. Always, the great mother has gone before you and knows what you are up against. She wants you to feel her presence and do your best.

For some of us, we need look no farther than the present to find out what makes us happy. Do we like to write? Play or listen to music? If we aren't sure, we can take some classes at a community college or Y. A young mother whose child entered first grade this year had no idea what she wanted for herself but felt she had disappointed her college music teacher by not wanting a career playing the violin. She had the talent for playing but not the heart for it. Now, with the first free time she had had in years, she signed up for yoga for her body, ceramic sculpture for creative expression, anger management for emotional release, and an art history class for her mind. She thought she'd drop whatever class didn't suit her, but they were all just perfect, she said. She bought herself a beautiful cream-colored leather journal and finished each day with a page she called "Here I Am" where she wrote about self-learning for the day.

How can we now let go of controlling our real selves and develop what we really were meant to be? We start with what we can remember of our natural selves. Some of us are lucky enough to have memories of our full energy and the activities that made us sing. It is important to write these memories down. Tell your story. Tell it to a friend, a therapist, a minister, a neighbor, but tell it. Listen to what you are saying. What did you like to do then? What stopped you? What sometimes brings those feelings back? Start a "real self" section in your journal and, whenever you feel you've tapped into a feeling that is your natural self, write about it.

Sometimes the natural self is hidden and must be coaxed back to life. Sometimes the natural self must be developed. Just as we must take time to get to know another person, we must take time to get to know ourselves.

To help in not controling your emotions, just think of water from a faucet and let it leak. Save full blast for when you're ready for a downpour. Right now you are just washing your hands of old controlled ways.

Note to the Reader: We're working on some core issues of self-identity this week. I've included seven possible exercises. If you possibly can, give yourself a gift of a sixty-minute writing period today.

Exercises

1. Think of the last time you compared yourself to someone and found yourself better. If you named the other and yourself, what names would you give? Miss Showing Too Much and Miss Just Right? Write down your own labels.

   Now, make up labels with a time you found yourself wanting. What were you feeling insecure about? What was the judge trying to do for you? What new name might help you let go of any comparison and perfectionism?

2. Light a candle and set some quiet time aside to reflect and write out the answers to these questions.

   ◆ Who am I?

   ◆ When I watch children at a park or playground, what do I like? How do they remind me of myself? How am I different?

   ◆ If I could do anything I wanted for one year, what would I do? Write down the answer in detail starting with an ideal day. Now explore the year and how it opens to you. Use *listmaking* and *streaming*.

   ◆ From the question above, name what qualities you would be using or developing in doing these things. How does that reflect your values?

   ◆ What other activities would strengthen these qualities? (For instance, self-initiative could be utilized in many situations.)

   ◆ What are three things I like best about myself?

   ◆ What are three things I like in others?

   ◆ What would I like to develop more of in myself?

   ◆ What are three things I want people to remember about me?

   ◆ What makes me feel good when I reflect over my day?

   ◆ Finish the sentence, "I'm happy when _____."

   ◆ What makes me angry?

3. Name three pleasurable life experiences. What did they teach you about yourself? Name three difficult life experiences. What did you learn about yourself?

4. Ask three friends who you are. Write out and reflect on their answers.

5. Sometimes someone comes into our lives and this person brings us closer to ourselves. Who has been an important mirror for you and what qualities did they bring out in you? How did that help you recognize yourself as you let go of old ways of thinking about yourself?

6. Do a *cluster* using the word *perfection*. What other words appear? What do these words mean to you?

7. Write down any sensitive areas that result from criticism and an affirmation for each one. (An affirmation is a short and positive message to yourself such as "I am just the right size for me.")

DAY 3: INTERRUPTING THE NEED TO CONTROL OTHERS

"Whereas I formerly believed it to be my bounden duty to call other persons to order, I now admit that I need calling to order myself."

—Carl Jung

I have a friend who says if she didn't control things around the house, things would go to the dogs. I see how nervous and angry she is at her family and I wonder if the dog's life isn't better. Or at least wouldn't some kind of exploring a different way help her spirit? What a relief if we could let go of control. Imagine the hardships we bring to ourselves and others when we don't.

We control for many reasons: to avoid being alone, fear of failure, to be right, to fix a situation, to be efficient and profitable. We might control to lessen our feelings or to be the boss and not feel vulnerable. It is always helpful to notice the times when we feel controlling and write what feelings bring about our controlling behavior.

We all want to be safe. To be in control can give us false security. It's as if we can make sure nothing bad will happen. We can nurture the part of us that is frightened of change by calming self-talk, writing, and prayer. We can ask the part of us that wants to control to unclench its hands. "Just this once," we might say to ourselves, "see what happens if I don't direct this." Let the family squabble while we eat the meal before us. Leave the table when it's enough nonsense and go to the other room. Act on what you may have said before coming and leave early. Go home and write a poem about separate lives connected by a silver twine. Try different solutions, appreciate your flexibility.

A client of mine had a friend who seemed to be backing off from their relationship. She asked the friend if there was something wrong between them. When her friend said no, she decided to let the friend make the next move. She decided: If her friend called, it would be a nice treat; if she didn't, my client vowed to feel her feelings and write about her disappointment, about what not controlling this relationship could teach her. What's the wisdom in letting others do what they need to do? How could she think well of herself regardless of the outcome? In this way, she was able to take care of herself and let go of her expectations.

Kathy is a nurse who cares for her patients. She stays in touch with many of them after their discharge and often uses her therapy hour with me to talk about the inadequate treatment they receive at home. She gets upset thinking about their unmet need for a drive to their favorite park, to watch a favorite video, or for conversation. She focuses on all they don't have and has little energy for herself; she is becoming burned out on the job. When we focus on someone else's needs and let our own go, it is a signal that we are controlling others.

In exploring her background, we find the sadness Kathy felt watching an unstable mother, how she became the caretaker and tried to make things brighter for her mom. Kathy needs to do her best at work and then in the evenings develop a life; to do this she must start letting go of other's lives. She needs to allow her patients to find their self-sufficiency. She could use writing to find her own self-sufficiency.

Why must she focus on others? What is missing in herself? What does she need? When is she in spirit?

Before she helped anyone, I asked Kathy to ask herself (1) did they ask for her help, (2) is her helping empowering them or weakening them, and (3) did she have the energy to help just now. If the answer to any of the three questions was no, she was to focus on herself by writing down what she needed for herself. She was to see herself as a tree whose limbs were strong but whose roots needed more nourishment.

So how do we let go of the control and react differently? By recognizing the triggers. Let's take an example of a friend's irritating whining. Yes, whining is pretty annoying, but it must be an old trigger because it bothers us so much. Before we show our anger, we should take a few minutes and write about what whining reminds us of. We may realize whining triggers the memory of the whine of an older brother who always seemed to get his way. We remember how we felt neglected. We didn't feel special. The sibling had the attention and if we ever whined our parents got angry. Whining may trigger how we'd have liked to be a whiney child ourselves sometimes, and how angry it makes us feel to always have to be the helper.

After you've written down what whining triggers in you, spend some time reassuring the part of you that feels neglected or negated that you are special, too. Talk to the child you once were with kindness. Promise her it is different today. Now you have choices. Ask your wise voice for guidance. Write a "super hero" ending to an old story that didn't change back then.

For now, remember that you are this person's friend by choice and you don't have to do things a certain way. You can react differently by taking the irritation out of your voice. You can give a suggestion and say it nicely. Remember, there is no child here and no mother. You can choose to say nothing and move on to another topic of conversation. You can decide not to help and remove yourself from the room.

You can tell your friend that whining triggers something in you, but that you love him and want him to feel better. Or you can tell him it's triggering an old feeling and you'd like to talk to him about the trigger later. You can ask him to stop. You can humor him. It's up to you.

If you want to change a controlling behavior, the process of tracing the feeling back to earlier times, finding the cause, reassuring the child, and finding new solutions can be helped by writing.

"Be kind; everyone you meet is fighting a hard battle."

—*John Watson*

Exercises

1. Think of a recent time when you wanted to control someone's behavior. Use the process of tracing the feeling back to earlier times. What was going on then? How did you feel? What did you need? What would help you feel better? Now look at the recent event and see how you could have reacted differently. Use *streaming* to explore this.

2. List emotional reactions you have toward a friend, a partner, a child, a family member, a co-worker, a neighbor. How would you like to react differently than you have in the past? What would your new reactions show that you are developing?

3. Dedicate a page in your journal for new, less controlling behaviors. Cut out images of happy, carefree people who are happy in the moment and glue them to the edges of the page. Write about these new behaviors.

DAY 4: LETTING GO OF NEGATIVITY

So often we live life thinking something's missing. We raise our children waiting for mothering to be over, we work at the office waiting for five o'clock, we picnic waiting to get home and be alone. Well, maybe something *is* missing. We can dialogue on the truth of that, but if we can get out of the habit of thinking that something better is about to happen, we will be more content. Life as it is meant to be is happening and there is enough good in it.

"It doesn't hurt to be optimistic. You can always cry later."

—*Lucimar Santos de Lima*

A friend of mine, Sharon, recently had to put her mother into a home for women with Alzheimer's. Her mother becomes agitated because she can't remember why she's in the home. To help her, Sharon wrote her a note in large, clear print. The note explains how Sharon had found her mother lying on the floor after a fall. She had lain there for two days. The note explained how they had found this home so she could be cared for and her children could come regularly to see her. Sharon's mother loves that note. She reads it several times a day and it reminds her of the good reasons she is in the home.

When we begin to explore letting go of control, we may begin to confront our own negative thinking. We notice what's wrong first. We expect it to be hard. We expect to fail. We are shocked when we go over old journals and see this negativity. We have spent so much time worrying over things that never happened! Now let us use our writing to move us out of negative thinking.

I remember when a friend gave up smoking. Every time she had smoking thoughts or cravings, she'd get up and go to the window and look for green and growing things. She used writing to release her negative feelings and to remind herself nonsmoking was what she wanted.

Our spirit life includes red tulips in the garden, chicken and corn on the cob, times of not enough money, and the feelings of not enough love. Not every year of our life will we have a best friend. Some days are made up of the overcooked casserole, junk mail, the restless night. The mundane is all right. It teaches us joy for days when we lay down a blanket and love. Good things take their time the way a meal needs simmering. Even the first drawings of a child may have arms coming out of heads or legs sprouting mouths and eyes, spatial relationships still shimmering in their forming brain.

. . . .

How the days launder us if we are sincere about living life in a way
that we value. We can be young and foolish, following radio dreams
and surf, wanting poetry and licorice nights. You may be allowed to
stay awhile in the dark forest, but the spirit will give you signals and
ask if this is what you want. It is okay to want good for yourself and
all others. It is okay to expect good to happen. Spend a moment
now feeling the wise speaking self who wants you to believe in her
and vow to follow the help she offers you.

Commit to choosing joy and aliveness. Let go of
negativity. Try to remember being very young and
having no thought but the game of hide-and-seek that
you were playing. No thought of growing to fourteen,
twenty-one. Laughter, that's what you were. Ponies of
laughter galloping through the neighborhood.

*"I have found if you love life, life will love
you back."*
—*Arthur Rubinstein*

Exercises

1. If you could see love as a tangled nest, swamp grass
   with coin and feather, love braided with fire, how could you better
   accept love in your life?

2. Make up little rhyming ditties to say to yourself when you are feeling negative. For example: Pity pot me, I'll go touch a tree. Or:
   Only wise me is free to be.

3. Spend a few minutes listing the good you have in your life and
   what this does for your spirit.

DAY 5: ACCEPTING AND REACHING FOR SUPPORT

The other day a man smiled kindly at me as I took his turn at a four-way stop. I wasn't trying to outdo him; I was daydreaming. He let it be and didn't shame me with gestures. I felt a sweep of connection to him and my spirit. His gentleness helped me remember my soul and to let go of my daily worry. I wrote a letter of thanks to him in my journal and wrote down other supportive things strangers had done.

I've had times in my life when I didn't know how I was going to support myself and my son. A kind face at the cleaners admittedly couldn't solve my problems, but the gentleness lifted my spirits and left me feeling less alone. There have been times when I was most acutely feeling love's bleeding heart and a child would hand me his toy and turn my mood to one of trust and community. The child would remind me of my wise speaking voice that says we are all a part of humanity.

This letting go process can sometimes leave us feeling vulnerable and alone. Sometimes feeling connected to a friend is all that's needed to feel better. We need to step back from our inner trembling and trust that other people like us and want us. A friend once told me it was nurturing just to have me in the same room. It was something I'll never forget, and I am delighted that she experiences my support in this way. She is one of my teachers.

Sometimes we don't ask for help because to do so feels like a blow

"Kindness is the golden chain by which society is bound together."

—*Johann von Goethe*

to our ego. We don't know the way but we don't want to ask for directions. We try circling around to find the street one more time. Other times the internalized voices ring loudly and we are afraid of showing vulnerability and need.

Take a chance. If you ask kind people, you have a good chance of getting the support you deserve. Try to ask for what you need right in the heart of things. Learn to look for who can be with you in a loving way. You deserve to have your muse stroked and made happy by the people you know. You'll feel better about your connection to others and will begin to trust others, too. Today our writing will help support us as we explore the old triggers, the expectations of being humiliated for having needs.

To ask for support is to ask your spirit to help you on your way. Your soul is supported by all the souls in the world. A client had been traveling on an around-the-world ticket. When she came home she looked out her attic window and saw the big dipper. She was jolted into awareness that everywhere we are supported by the stars that shine. Her traveling memories were important, the faces of people around the world and their customs, but nothing was more impressive than to think of the way she was soulfully supported. She wove stories of connection through her journal and prayed them in her evening prayers.

This is what God loves. People finding happiness in spirit. Our actions and friends supporting us. People drawing close.

Imagine a safe world where our spirit rests, where sleep and dreaming support us. When the day comes, watch the clouds grace the land with shadows to ease the throw of sun. Let the warmth of our home lift any tilt of sorrow, the cool of the late afternoon breeze reminds us that we are not alone. Let the world support our life with all its puppies and ducks and gentle sounds.

Know that even the powerful sea can't stay in one place for long. Change happens. Sometimes we won't feel supported. We need to check to see if we have spilled ourselves into activities and away from our spirit. If so, let it be a short journey back to ourselves.

59

Exercises

1. Dialogue with a person in your life who would support you or once did support you. How did it strengthen your connection? Now think of a time you helped someone. How did it strengthen your connection?

2. Think of your life today and write down what you might need help with at work, socially, a personal project, a child, your spiritual development. Now list those who might help you and what you might ask them to do.

DAY 6: SURRENDER

I dreamt that I wanted a great force to help me so I shook a nearby chestnut tree to get God down, get him closer, to take care of me. The harder I shook, the more leaves fell and the barer the tree was. I didn't know it at the time, but I was being taught a lesson in letting go of control. I couldn't force spirit to come into my life, but I could create a tree without leaves unable to give shade.

"When nothing is sure, anything is possible."
—*Margaret Drabble*

I never thought of letting go of control as a positive thing until I became an adult. I had never thought of giving up on purpose and asking the spirit for help. Giving up of any sort seemed a shameful thing to do. I couldn't imagine giving up my power, relinquishing my control. It was admitting defeat and laziness to willingly surrender my life to a God to see what the day might bring. What kind of industry was that!

Once, just before I interviewed for a position as an administrator of an arts organization, I sewed a button on my purple raincoat. Halfway through the interview, it occurred to me that I hadn't cut the needle and thread and tied the knot. I went through the interview wondering what was hanging on my chest. Because it hadn't rained and I wasn't wet and the room was cold, I undid my coat but left it on. Finally, I couldn't bear it anymore and I looked down. Yes, the needle and thread were hanging there, more in my lap than on my chest. I smiled at the board members and they smiled back. I'll never know if anyone noticed, but I got the job. I was powerless and just let go of control. What a reminder of the importance of surrender.

"Move, beat your drums, cry, disturb your powerlessness until it shifts to inspiration." —Jan Alice Pfau

Do you remember having a toothache and checking it out with your tongue or checking to see if your neck still hurt by jerking your neck to feel it more. We can worry a problem like a tooth. There is a time to reflect on a concern, a time to get feedback, a time to take action, and a time to let it go.

This letting go is the action that leads to surrender. We can write about the long ribbon of life that precedes us and goes on after us. We may reach our limit and realize there is nothing else to do and worry is of no help. We may remember that we worry ourselves practically to death and then always feel a calm after all that emotion when we let go. We can write, "I am powerless. I can do nothing more. I let go and surrender this to the powers that be."

It can be difficult to surrender and see what happens next. Our can-do culture emphasizes the importance of action. Surrender may look like passivity. Yet surrender is being awake and with full intention of taking care of whatever problem is facing you. It is saying to your muse, "Help me understand more than I do now. Let me know what to do," and giving yourself time to write.

Surrender leads to spiritual growth because it reminds us we are part of a larger picture. We can do our part and yet we don't know how our life fits into the whole. Philosopher Alan Watts, on his tape *Out of the Trap*, lectures about how at the moment you are wondering

"Let me stand with my age with all its waters flowing around me. If they sometimes subdue, they must finally upbear me, for I seek the universal—and that must be the best."
—Margaret Fuller

what to do next, the world is listening. You are part of the world, and your wondering what to do is part of what makes the world at that moment. The world could not be that if you were not wondering. To be that moment, everything had to be the way it was.

Watts reminds us in his wonderful way that things are the way they are at any moment because you are doing what you are doing. This made me feel more part of things and better able to let go of trying to control my doubt. I could choose to put hope into the mix of the world. This idea helped me surrender just a little more.

Surrender is easier if you can imagine that your body does not hold your soul. Rather, your soul holds your body. This thought reminds us that the soul is everything we are. All there really are are our souls in the world. Our spiritual path connects us to everything there is. When we surrender to this truth, we understand the universe is souls touching, everything in its place, and that there is much we don't know. We do our footwork and surrender in prayer. We write and ask our wise speaking voice to help us.

Exercises

1. Think about how you feel physically or emotionally when you are passive. When you are surrendering. Write about these different states.

2. Look out your window and see what part of nature is surrendering right now. Explore what that does for the world and you.

3. Imagine yourself on a swing, your arms high on the thick rope. Think of your arms as high in surrender to movement, gravity, the powers that be. What concern needs help beyond your will? How could you use prayer to help yourself?

DAY 7: REWARDING YOURSELF— FLOWING WITH THE WATER

Take yourself to a body of water and ask the water to pour its wisdom over you. Use *streaming* to learn from water's qualities what you need to live with. *Cluster* about something living in water. *Dialogue* with the teacher of the water.

"My old friend, water, my good companion, my beloved mother and father; I am its most natural offspring."

—Doris Grumbach

WEEK 4: THE FULL RIVER

ℭℓ Trusting Our Knowledge

Our culture encourages logical thinking, which theorizes that we do things to get a certain result. Logical thinking is helpful in many ways. And there are times when it is not only helpful, but it can make us feel a certain way. First you take step one, then step two, then step three—yes, we can all agree and off we go.

The problem is that logical thinking doesn't take into account the unexpected or nonsensical world. It supposes that by doing things logically we stay in control. If you've ever tried to talk to someone who was only aware of his logic, you'll know exactly what I mean. It is not a satisfying experience. You can't talk about feelings or human nature, you can't explain why you take teeny-tiny bits of string and lay it on a broken spider web to re-create the world of nature. Art doesn't make sense to a purely logical mind.

Neither does spirit. Spirituality is intellectual, but it's not logical. So much that we value about ourselves and the world is outside the sphere of logic. As we learn from living, life is not always logical. Things happen that don't make sense. In *Hare Brain, Tortoise Mind*, Guy Claxton appeals to us to be less analytical and to let our creativity have a freer rein. Creativity will factor in our hurts, desires, and dreams. A recent best-seller, *Emotional Intelligence* by Daniel Goleman, confirms what our wise voice has long known: We receive information in many ways, not just through the rational, logical mind. This week we'll focus on developing our inner knowing.

We listen to a person speak and learn from his tone. We watch him talk to us and we obtain more information. Sometimes we sense his words aren't congruent with his actions. Occasionally, someone will be able to taste something sour when spoken to by a boss. Some people smell something odorous when they are being lied to. These are examples of how the body's senses can help you understand the information you are receiving.

"Intuition is a spiritual faculty and does not explain, but simply points the way."

—*Florence Scovel Shinn*

Intuitive knowledge may be a flash of knowing what we can trust, even respect, but we must be able to recognize the feeling. For instance, we've been looking for a house to rent. When we walk into the living room of a prospective home, the light is pouring through the side window. Before we tour the rest of the house, we see our comfortable chair at the window. It's our new place and we know it.

We can release feelings of being overwhelmed in our lives by trusting that we can handle what happens to us. By trusting ourselves and our responses we become happy to be alive. We then have a chance to work and play and look up at the stars.

Our writing can help us find our center. I tell my clients: Good decisions are made when we are in balance. Balance is won not by the absence of conflict but by the presence of our wise self. Unless we find balance in ourselves we cannot find it anywhere else.

DAY 1: RECEIVING KNOWLEDGE THROUGH OUR EMOTIONS

"Many people would rather die than think. In fact they do."

—*Bertrand Russell*

There's a saying in the recovery movement that if we could have thought it through by now, we would have. Thinking will take us many places, but sometimes we have to rely on our emotions and other body sensations to get to our deeper truth.

Emotions are our global subject responses at a given moment. They are distinct from any body feelings that may be going on at the same time and distinct from the behaviors they generate and the value judgments we make about them. They are messages. An emotionally healthy person can identify her feelings, respond to any given situation with emotions that are most appropriate and useful, and express her feelings honestly. For instance, she can tell the difference between disappointment and frustration, anger and sadness.

I can think of a time when I had a negative emotional response to someone and ignored the signals. I just tried harder to be pleasant and found myself drained and without good connection. What I had forgotten is that within us there are wells of thought and emotion and energy about which we are not aware. What I needed to do in that situation was trust how I felt, for otherwise I'd be acting in opposition to my spirit. But first I had to really *know* how I felt.

Writing allows us to record this process of coming to know how we feel and trusting our feelings. It allows us to pinpoint the journey to the spirit, the emotional signals, the ups and downs. It gives us a record to go back to so we can see how far we've come. It also helps us keep a record of those core issues that will take a lifetime to work through.

Through our writing, we can enter the sacred realm and find there the meaning of grace. We can feel the words spill on our feelings and calm us until we can hear the spirit voice.

"Writing. It's like striking a match. Sometimes it lights."

—*Neil Simon*

Exercises

1. Remember a time when you felt disappointed and another when you felt frustrated. What was the difference? What were the signals? What were the best responses to each?

2. In *The Emotional Hostage*, Leslie Cameron-Bandler suggests we name six emotions we would like to experience for the rest of our life

and six to do away with. Try this out in your journal and see what your wise speaking person says.

3. Using the techniques of *gazing into the waters* and then *streaming,* write what activities make you feel happy.

DAY 2: BODY SENSATIONS AND INTUITION

Our bodies are alive with clues to help us trust ourselves. It is only in this culture that we try to think of ourselves as separate from feeling and body. Yet the spirit lives in all three realms.

An example of trusting your body sensations might be when you get a call from an office where you've applied for work, but after talking to the manager, your stomach is tight. You decide you'll go to a networking group instead and get some other leads. This is paying attention to the intuitive kinesthetic sense in your body.

Sometimes we can envision what will happen by relaxing and taking time to ask our spirit. As we *dialogue* in writing, we might hear a voice softly tell us something we need to hear. We may taste success. What matters is that you are alive to the possibility of trusting your senses.

You may feel a vibration in your body, warning you to be cautious, or another signaling that you should be open to new possibilities. Sometimes a particular body part is your reliable source. For me, it's my stomach. I've had clients whose knees ache when they need to say no, and others whose wrists are their guide. I once worked with a man whose itching nose was a sign that something good was about to happen.

"If you let your fear of consequence prevent you from following your deepest instinct, then your life will be safe, expedient and thin."

—*Katharine Butler Hathaway*

A woman who was raised by a manic-depressive father came to me wanting to trust herself, but she wasn't sure how to do it. She had never been able to count on her father's reactions to be predictable or helpful and needed someone she could trust to give her feedback about her thoughts and feelings. I asked how she knew she could trust me. She said she guessed it was because after taking a workshop with me, her heart felt open. She had listened and watched me and felt safe. Her body knew.

We did a visualization of a place in which she knew she would feel safe. At first she was in a tiny boat and was sailing the sea. The sea was calm and she was safe. Soon the boat felt too small, since it could only hold her and she wanted to be with others. She saw herself in a garden. She was in the garden with her closest friend. She could smell the lilies of her grandmother's garden and knew that she had found a safe place to envision herself when she felt anxious and unsure.

I asked her if I could be nearby and the smell of lilies intensified for her. She knew that I was in her grandmother's heart, she said. (Later, her father said she should have peeked to see if I had sprayed a scent into the room.) She felt she could count on her sense of smell. Although I know that the olfactory sense is often very strong, this was one of the few times I've seen a client rely on smell as an intuitive sign. Now when she's in doubt about what to do, she'll relax, think of possible solutions, and sense their smell.

We learn to trust our body's signals by putting the information into practice. If you sense that a friend will get an important letter next week, call her at the end of that week and ask if she received something important in the mail. If your belly says to forgive your sister and you call her and you feel lighter, remember the belly feeling. Next time you want to know what to do and the belly feels the same way, it may be a sign to be proactive. In time, you can sense yes as well as no.

Sometimes we have an intuitive feeling about a situation that tells us it's not time to act yet. My friend Rosemary earns good money as a corporate trainer and wanted to leave her roommate situation and get a place of her own with a large room for an office. She had paid off her school debts and had a small but comfortable savings account. She felt that the move was the right thing to do, but the timing seemed wrong and she couldn't understand why. She waited to see if this would become clearer. Two weeks later she received a call asking if she would come to Chicago for a year to work for a company she had been courting and had given up on. She knew immediately she would maintain her present living situation so she could return and see friends during the year; she would move into her own place once her contract with the firm in Chicago was completed. She was glad she trusted the intuitive feeling that told her it wasn't the time for her to get her own place.

"Enoch never nagged his blood to tell him a thing until it was ready."
—Flannery O'Connor

By trial and error, we can learn to trust our intuition. We can remember what the inklings that either lead us toward or away from something felt like. We can distinguish between the two feelings until we are sure of our hunches. By paying attention to the small things first, we can learn to trust our intuition for the big ones. We can develop an intuitive knowledge about both healthy and harmful people and situations.

Just be aware of all the ways you absorb information and trust that knowledge however it comes to you. You are not one-dimensional. You are a sculpture in motion and are given body sensations, the ability to think, to have emotions and intuition as a resource to your knowing.

"I have gotten back to the old ways. This happened as I began to have visions; I was drawn back to the old ways by them. I did not choose it outwardly; it came as I released old ways of being, its irresistible call bringing me home."

—Brooke Medicine Eagle

Exercises

1. Write down the times when you had a premonition that something would happen and it did. Or write down the times when you felt something would be good or dangerous and it turned out to be true. How did you know? What are your primary intuitive senses? How do they signal you?

2. What keeps you away from trusting your body's reactions? *Listmake* those barriers. How can you trust your body more?

3. Scan a few magazines and see what the pictures are intuitively saying to you. Write down the messages you get from the pictures you are drawn to as you think of healing the past. Listen to what the wise speaking person says.

DAY 3: RELEASING OVERWHELM

Kara felt overwhelmed and wanted to use hypnotherapy to calm herself. She was a beautiful woman who was ending a ten-year-long relationship. She felt her husband wanted her to be his trophy wife. He worked seven days a week and didn't talk to her. She became *"Then again, maybe I won't."* —*Judy Blume* aware that she had known in the first year of their relationship that she wasn't satisfied, but had denied her loneliness by staying busy. She didn't want to get divorced partly because of her religion. She wanted to make the difficult choice her intuition was telling her to make so she could like herself again, but she was frightened of the coming losses. After relaxation with hypnotherapy, she realized she could continue to hold and work toward her dream of a happy marriage, but it would have to be with a different mate.

After ten years of unhappiness, Kara knew more of what she didn't want than what she did. She used writing and her wise speaking voice to get to know what made her happy. She wanted to feel better connected to the world and began to use streaming to explore what she had liked in each of her jobs. She explored what job might hold these qualities. She did the same for what kind of product she wanted to work with and what qualities she liked in a boss. She began a wise-man section of her journal and wrote down the qualities she felt most connected to in men. She kept a list of the wise men in her life and added to this list whenever she could.

Kara's story illustrates some of the obstacles we throw up when we are overwhelmed: fear of what others will think, denying feelings, postponing the nasty daily tasks, and not trusting that we won't always feel this bad. It's hard to trust ourselves or our intuition when

"At work, you think of the children you have left at home. At home, you think of the work you've left unfinished. Such a struggle is unleashed within yourself. Your heart is rent."

—*Golda Meir*

we're overwhelmed. We can all remember times when we had an important decision to make and didn't feel sure we were doing the right thing because so much was coming at us at once. Listmaking can help us figure out what's what. By writing down all that needs to be done we can prioritize and decide what we must do first. Fears may surface, but we can sit quietly and use our writing time to explore our fears. We may be afraid to move forward with the things that need to be done or we may be afraid not to. It's important to listen to these feelings. For example, anxiety may be an important signal about something in your future for which you need to prepare. It may also be a habitual response of only seeing disaster. By writing, we can give considered thought to our feelings and see if we can't affect change in a good way. Try it! It will help.

Sometimes our body tells us we need to grieve. We need to honor grief and give it room and time to happen. Manda felt a tight knot in her heart after her best friends moved. She felt overwhelmed with making the adjustment to live her daily life without them. She felt sorry for herself for being single. She felt tears behind her eyes but couldn't cry. She went to a little neighborhood theater showing old classics the week of their move. The movies changed each night and she was there every night in the same seat with the same snack of popcorn and root beer. Finally she had a good cry and could feel her loss. She was then able to reach out to others. She trusted her body signals of grief and gave herself time to release these feelings. The tears in the movies helped her release enough grief so she could return to her journal and not feel so numb. Then, writing helped her continue exploring her loneliness.

Uri was hosting a small party where he was reciting a poem by Mary Oliver. He had lost his job and had memorized poetry between interview preparations. Mary was his favorite. He was drawn to the beauty of the language and it calmed him during a time that could have been overwhelming to him. When he found a new job he called his friends and invited them to dinner; he also told them to bring a favorite poem. He recited the poem "Wild Geese" by Mary Oliver, which tells us we are part of the world of human animals and do not have to be a certain way. Uri followed his emotional feelings and let poetry be a solace to him. He continued writing in his journal but now added inspirational poetry to help him on his way.

When you feel overwhelmed, start a dialogue with your wise self. Ask your intuition for help. Tell at least one person how it really is for you. Ask the deep forest how you can be rescued. Pray for intuitive guidance. Whenever you're not sure of how you feel, use your writing to gain clarity.

There is an old Yiddish proverb that says, "God gave us burdens, also shoulders." What we need is within us, and we can find our way through writing. Remember, we have what we seek. With time and attention, it will surface.

Exercises

1. Write a free verse poem using several metaphors to describe your feelings. Let metaphors describe what you want or what is happening. Let metaphors tell you how it's been for you in the past. End your poem by getting what you want. Here's an example:

> Her voice is a plain, the flat
> land of our country's flax. I can count
> on her. Her trust in me is satin,
> reaches long and soft and lovely.
>
> I weave between the treacherous
> paths that call me back
> to the tunnel, nights in the cave.
> I twist in the tumbled sheets I sleep in.
>
> Who are we and why have we stumbled here?

2. Find a picture that seems reassuring. What does it remind you of? How is that reassuring? What does it seem to teach you?

3. Sometimes changing a passage of prose to poetry can make you feel your feelings more. Try it.

DAY 4: DEVELOPING CLARITY

There is a form of meditation from Tibet that helps us pause and remember ourselves. To remember ourselves gives us clarity. Clarity happens when our thoughts are focused, our feelings calm. When our body feels like a vessel that can easily hold us and we know what direction we're going. I like this meditation because unlike the traditional mind meditations that ask us to follow the breath or stare at a candle, this one gives us time to pause and feel our emotions. From this feeling state, many people find it easier to write.

Peace Meditation

"Much sheer effort goes into avoiding truth: left to itself, it sweeps in like the tide."

—Fay Weldon

The Peace Meditation helps us to experience our feelings rather than watch what our mind does. Those feelings are connected to our self-knowledge. This meditation leans on the pause and lets us keep in touch with our body and its breath but gives us room to feel.

1. Notice the *out breath*. Say "old" as you breathe out. This releases us from the past.

2. Now notice the *in breath*. The in breath gives you time to pause between out breaths; it gives you time to experience your feelings. The in breath is an opening. It helps you practice patience. Notice how expanded you feel.

When you sit down to write after doing the Peace Meditation, you will often experience a sudden clarity that's been troubling you for some time. For instance, you might explore in writing a concern in your original family and realize that what is currently going on is not your concern. It is between your father and your brother. The emotional knowledge that was accessed through the meditation brings a feeling of less family responsibility and more self-responsibility.

When you're feeling unclear, sitting with your feelings and writing about them can be of enormous help. You might try listing all the reasons for doing one thing and then the other. Then simply surrender until intuitive clarity comes. This clarity often comes while concentrating on something else. This is no accident. The intuitive mind speaks most clearly when you relax your thinking mind.

"I use my hands like a sculpture, to mold and shape the sound I want to clarify." —Leonard Slatkin

After struggling to get just the right ending to a poem and not succeeding, I take a break and do the dishes, or talk to a friend about the movies, or take a walk. At some point during my mind's break, the ending for the poem may come.

Exercises

1. Imagine a bubble of clarity. This is where you can reside. Nothing bothers you here in this magical quiet. The guardian angel watches over you as you enter and rest. Use *streaming* and write down your experience.

2. Meditate using the *out breath* to say "old" and the *in breath* to feel a pause. After five minutes, write about your process of doing this. How close to peace did you come? Can you trust that peace is always within you whether you feel it or not? How do peace and clarity join together to help you get in touch with your soul's message?

3. Write with found images and objects. Directly observe and write what they say about finding clarity.

DAY 5: STANDING UP FOR WHAT WE BELIEVE

"And the trouble is,
if you don't risk anything,
you risk even more."

—Erica Jong

My experience is that when I trust myself, I can more easily do the right thing for myself. So when I trust myself it's quite natural to follow a value system of treating others with kindness yet not forgetting to include myself in this equation. I know my wise speaking self wants consideration for all. I'll ask you to join me for a movie when I know you're lonely, but I won't go to a violent action movie no matter what. I'll be generous with my time if you show up late, but if we make new plans, I'll ask for a specific meeting time.

We use our thinking, emotions, and intuition to find the way to our truth. We consider what our spirit wants for us. We consider what it means to be human. We sort out our values of spirit and humanness so we know how we want to be when in relationship to others, our work, and the way we live our lives. Self-knowledge give us courage to stand up for what we believe. The belief in our spirit life helps us learn to trust our decisions.

In her book *Loving in the War Zone*, Cherrie Moraga writes a poem about being caught in the war in Nicaragua. Trying to outrun the soldiers, she considers leaving her lover behind to outrun the soldiers. She could outrun the soldiers and have a better chance of escape. However, what would her life be like if she were the kind of person who deserted her loved one? She chose to escape with her lover even though this slowed her down. Miraculously, they made it to freedom. She could take this action because she trusted herself and her value system and acted accordingly.

"I believe one writes
because one has to create
a world in which
one can live."

—Anaïs Nin

Sometimes standing up for what you believe is as simple as slowing down for a minute and getting a sense of what is intuitively best for you. What would make your spirit glad to be you? Should you cheat to make sure you win, or should you simply do your best? What would cheating mean to your spirit? What would winning or failing mean to your spirit? Sometimes society encourages us to go against our spirit and we must remember why we choose to live.

Our journals are a great place for dialoguing with ourselves. Name the conflict and then dialogue about it. Sometimes the answer isn't immediate. The last time a friend did this she told me the answer was to take a few days off and ask herself again afterward.

Every time a person follows his own drummer he helps even the most unexamined member of society take a deeper breath. It's because a person who finds freedom to be himself puts a touch of freedom's energy in the soul of all of us. He gives us possibility.

It helps to have role models we respect who follow their self-knowledge. I remember a colleague listening to a student try to convince him to give her special treatment. He'd listen with his arms open and his feet firm on the ground, his head tilted toward the student to get a sense of what was going on; he asked questions and then say yes or no with a smile. It amazed me how he could trust himself in the moment. Using him as a role model, I gradually became able to do this myself.

You might be a baker. A wandering teacher of English as a second language. An insurance manager. You might choose to work in a large office, or at home, consulting. You might invent mechanical things in the garage. Or sell a service you believe in. The god force has many names. Hallowed be the names. Choose what's right for you.

In the movie *La Vie en Rose* (My Life in Pink), a young boy intuits that he is meant to be a girl. He tells everyone he was born in the wrong body. His family tells him to stop saying he's a girl, but he has great clarity. He is a girl. He is delighted when he learns about X and Y chromosomes and how that determines one's sex. He rushes to his parents to give them the explanation of his wrong gender; his other X was lost. It was a scientific mistake and now others, he hopes, can accept him as he accepts himself. In the end, it's his intuition that leads to answers of what is best.

Through our writing we can better figure out who we are and what we believe.

Exercises

1. Think of a movie or book where the hero or heroine takes a stand and does what he or she believes in. What was the action of the believer and the others? On what knowledge was the decision based? Write about how that made you feel.

2. Write down the ways you feel unsettled about conflict. How does this get in the way of taking a stand? Explore any unsettled feeling. How does this tie in with not wanting to stand out?

3. We all have stuff in our way. Imagine reaching inside your body and taking out any "unnecessary stuffing." What would it look like? What story does it tell?

DAY 6: FINDING BALANCE

I have a client who can hear crystal crashing in her mind when something is wrong. It's her intuitive warning bell. She's in management and doesn't say that that crystal just broke when she's sitting in a meeting. But she has acted on this source of information often enough to know she can trust it. It helps, she says, if she is not hung over and her head is clear.

"To be rooted is perhaps the most important and least recognized need of the human soul."

—Simone Weil

This same client uses her thinking and logical mind to predict sales patterns and to develop corresponding marketing plans. She checks those numbers and patterns against what she observes in the world. She lets herself take the time to see how she feels about what's happening or about to happen emotionally. (The emotional checking in helps her stay current with her happiness.) She's good at her job because she has learned to balance the different ways she receives knowledge and to honor them all.

Writing is one of life's great balancers. It gives us a place between the real world and the world of the imagination. A place where the two worlds meet. To sort through our troubles in writing gives us a chance to be a person with troubles but not a troubled person. Françoise Sagan is quoted as saying, "I shall live badly if I do not write, and I shall write badly if I do not live" (*New York Times* Book Review, 1956). Or we can learn from Joan Didion when she says that she writes entirely to find out what she's thinking, what she's looking at, what she sees, and what it means. What she wants and what she fears.

A writer friend recently told me he didn't know how to write the book he wrote until he was almost through. He thought it would be easy to write his second book, but once again he figured out how to write it only by doing it. So is it with life. We live and learn. We deepen the learnings by writing. It's a balance.

Balance allows us to concentrate on the here and now. You know when you are in balance because you are in the present day rather than reliving the past or worrying about the future. It's fine to look back or to the future when you are in therapy or being reflective, but most of the time we want to live our lives joyfully being with what or who is in front of us, the wind, the food, the friend, the book, the robin.

Some of us are energized by being with others. Others need lots of time to themselves to recharge. Whatever is your natural way, as you grow and mature, you will find a balance between your needs for engagement and solitude.

Just a word about addictions. You won't be able to trust yourself while you're relying on "spirits" from a bottle or any other substance. You must find balance by being willing to rely on the higher power or the goddess being. You tell your higher power that these are your feelings and ask for help to live with them. The choice is yours. Once you put down the substance and feel the power of spiritual living, you will realize you really haven't given up anything at all.

Exercises

1. Dialogue with the part of you that craves excitement. When have you felt joy? Now do some *streaming* and see what you can learn about yourself and what you need to remember about balance.

2. The answer to finding balance could be in little things. Make a schedule of small actions to do each day that help you find balance, such as writing in the morning, noticing your breath as you walk to work, checking in with your body to see if you need a break and how best to do that. Try keeping this schedule for a week.

3. Pick an object to which you have been emotionally attached in some way. How did that object help with your balance? Do you remember different times in your life when it was important to you? Describe them and see what they have to teach you.

DAY 7: REWARDING YOURSELF—
THE SPIRIT GROWS

All week you've been writing about trusting yourself by paying attention to the different ways you can determine what is right for you. Today, go to a local nursery and let yourself browse through the aisles and see what your senses say to you. How do you feel? Intuitively, what do you know about flowers? What does your spirit say about plants that must be planted annually or those that come back each year? How do you respond to the tiny seedlings compared to the larger plants? What does your reaction to seedlings tell you about how you trust?

"If I had but two loaves of bread, I would sell one and buy hyacinths, for they feed my soul."

—*Koran*

WEEK 5: THE SELF REBORN

Sense of Self

In *To Be Young, Gifted and Black*, Lorraine Hansberry explores the belief that everyone is dramatically interesting and a creature of stature. We each have our own story that is shaped by our race, gender, nationality, age, sexual preference, ethnicity, and psychological and spiritual awareness. We each have a right to our voice and we have one. The sense of self knows there is something unique about us since we are born one of a kind, alone.

Some people or experiences in your life may make you feel hesitant to express yourself fully. I can think of no better tool for exploring what your spirit is trying to tell you about your fears of harm and abandonment than writing.

Camille came from a family of college professors who looked down on her. I looked at the pretty forty-year-old before me and saw the pain in her face as she told me how invisible she felt. I also saw clear eyes and rosy red cheeks. I felt her strong sense of integrity.

She was a hands-on person who didn't do as well in school as her siblings. Looking back, she realized she wasn't interested in learning until she enrolled in a design school. Design was exciting to her and she did well. She was a very sensate person. Now she works as a pattern maker for a well-known fashion house. She loves measuring and cutting materials. She has found a job that suits her and one she likes.

Yet it's been hard to move beyond the opinions of her family. Every year she travels back to Baltimore to celebrate Passover with her family, and every year she finds herself in a depression. This year she decided to strengthen her belief in herself.

I helped Camille to visualize a chalkboard on which were written inappropriate labels from her youth. Camille saw the words *dumb, slow,* and *gullible.* In the visualization, she replaced them with the words *smart, precise,* and *honest.* The new labels were better reflections of who she was. She could remind herself of this. In time, she would tell her family about the new labels she had given herself and the harm the old labels had done.

Camille was living what she wanted for herself and not someone else's image or to make her parents happy. She was replacing her identification she had within her family with a sense of herself.

To choose yourself takes self-esteem and boundaries. "I want the freedom to carve and chisel my own face, to staunch the bleeding with ashes, to fashion my own gods out of my entrails," writes Gloria Anzaldua in *Borderlands.*

Honesty means telling ourselves our strengths and limitations and being willing to share these states. When we have a sense of self, we can be honest about it. The confusion lifts and we can say, "This is who I am. This is what I believe." We are what we are and that has value, this face, these bones, these feelings and opinions. Throughout this week we'll be using our writing time to explore how to be fully ourselves.

DAY 1: BEYOND IMAGE

Betty is a teacher who says she feels exposed because she wears her feelings on her sleeve. She says one bad night of worry or one good cry and even her young junior high students are asking if she is all right.

She wishes she could hide her feelings so she wouldn't be so vulnerable in hard times. But this is what others like about her. What you see is what you get. Betty presents no false persona or image. She is there before you just as she really is and that inspires people's trust. Her spirit is not hidden.

Rupert found that only his pleasant thoughts were acceptable in his family of origin. His parents got angry if he had problems, and he was admonished not to take risks. He now realizes that his parents didn't know how to guide him. They didn't know how to listen. He learned to appear as if everything was all right even when he was hurting. He learned to protect himself by projecting a competent image.

Now Rupert works in public relations and can use his pleasant personality and keep up a successful image for his job, but he has a tendency to isolate himself when he most needs to reach out for help. He often feels that people don't understand or like him. Rupert is realizing that others don't know him well because all they see is his "together" image.

Rupert has an easier time looking competent and calm than Betty does. However, in some personal ways, life is more difficult for him because he is more alone when despair comes. He has learned to use writing to express himself beyond his external image. He dialogues between his "image" and his "real self." Slowly, he is learning to recognize what he wants. Betty doesn't have much façade to hide and she lets her self show. Once she feels secure in her sense of self, she'll give up the struggle of concealment and let herself be loved or not. The important thing is that she loves herself.

Our external persona is not necessarily good or bad. As we have seen, it is often a survival mechanism, a self-protection. It can be helpful not to show every feeling. However, when this persona is constantly projected even around those with whom we want intimacy, it creates a wall. To be understood or loved, we need to show who we are underneath our external self. We don't want to be looked on as special, because the image of "specialness" separates us from others. What we want is to find a place among others. The wise person is asking you to find her and take a breath.

As a hypnotherapist, I sometimes deal with people who are caught behind a mask. As children, they felt rejected and learned to build a persona for protection. They often do not understand why people

"I'm Calamity Jane. Get the hell out of here and let me alone."
—Calamity Jane

"I did not lose myself all at once. I rubbed out my face over the years washing away my pain, the same way carvings on stone are worn down by water."
—Amy Tan

seem to dislike them or why they want to trip them up. They are told they seem phony to others and they don't understand what others want from them. They don't have the awareness to know they aren't expressing their real selves.

Robin was a management trainer in a large city on the East Coast for many years. Her co-workers found her competitive. They didn't trust her to work in the best interest of the group. It was hard to know what she really felt.

Robin was working hard to do her job of assessing needs, writing curriculum designs, and conducting training sessions. She believed people sometimes need to be sacrificed in order to get the job done. She'd get a great idea for a training and ram it through with no regard as to what someone else might be hoping to do. She would be agreeable to her co-workers, but behind their backs, she would be setting up a "win" for herself. She was a "do" machine with little awareness of who she really was. She could be whatever someone wanted her to be at that moment. She was a chameleon, changing who she was to fit the situation in order to win.

Often, someone like Robin needs to experience a failure and feel distress before she will explore who she is beneath the mask of the successful and achieving self. It can be frightening to realize she has almost totally forgotten who she is. The journey toward self takes a willingness to wander without understanding the calm place we are seeking.

We never mean to leave our inner voice behind. Sooner or later, the soul will find a way to call us back. There'll be a work failure or a relationship disappointment or an illness and we'll ask ourselves, "Who am I?" or "Where have I been?" Writing will be there for us asking us to sit quietly, pick up the pen, and be.

Exercises

1. Write down your self-hate messages, doubts, and fears. How do these affect your life? What could live beyond these messages?

2. Use *streaming* to explore how your external image has helped you and not helped you live your life. Now, using *dialoguing*, look at what is between your image and your real voice and see what a sense of self would feel like if it were authentic.

3. Write down and keep a list of the times when you have felt it safe to express yourself freely. A friend calls this a time when the living things crawl out. What helped you speak up? How do these moments affect your spiritual path?

DAY 2: CHANGING IDENTIFICATION

I recently taught a class on "Women and Money" in which we explored beliefs about money and how these beliefs are expressed by the way we handle money. We agreed that women are confused about money because their identities in this culture have changed since childhood. As we examine money, we examine our shifting identities. Through our writing we can explore why we keep money "fuzzy," the attitudes of our original family members toward money and how we have taken that on, and what we think of the successful person inside of us. We ask our wise person to be present in our explorations so that money and spirit can live together.

"No sooner do we think we have assembled a comfortable life than we find a piece of ourselves that has no place to fit in."
—Gail Sheehy

I have a friend who never wanted to be a wife and mother. She loves working with her creative muse and never thought to do anything else. She is a metalsmith by training and makes lamps that are like shamanistic shadow boxes. She has a partner, friends, and wonderful work. She's happy and fulfilled. She allowed herself to differ from the norm, to break with common gender roles. She is living in spirit.

Men, too, have to cope with changing roles, and this affects their expression of self. What happens to the image of the man-in-charge when he is asked to co-operate equally with his partner? How can he feel like a good person when more and more people decry the system of white male privilege. What is his spiritual path?

Ben is an analytical and kindhearted thirty-five-year-old attorney who works for a midsize law firm. He and his two sisters were raised by a feminist mom and openhearted father. He understands his privilege and also has his own issues about fitting in with the firm's lawyers. He immediately notices by reading body language the way the men tense when a woman or minority enters the room. The conversations and behavior also become more guarded and less playful.

Ben decided to help one person at a time. First he helped a minority woman get hired as an attorney and keep her job by allying with her in meetings just enough until she was more accepted by the other men. He offered a Hispanic man help in understanding the firm's system of getting things processed efficiently and provided ongoing advice on how to deal with the bureaucracy. He encouraged an older "temp" woman to apply for a permanent opening.

Ben didn't have the confidence to confront his peers and bosses directly, but he found a way to live soulfully. He says he's not much of a journal keeper, but when confronted with a difficult situation he does write down the pros and cons to possible solutions. He feels the need to know what his choices are and how he feels even if he doesn't express himself directly. Ben is doing the best he can by the actions he takes, and that is soulful.

Our soul houses the lively spirit of exploration and expression. We can't always see the outcome of our expression but we can try to take the risk to express ourselves. We can accept the responsibility and understand how we are affected by our society and histories and take measures to let our spirits talk. We can understand and accept how shifting identities shape our lives, and that brings us to loving ourselves more. We can forgive ourselves for what we don't do well or easily. We can find the best ways to express ourselves and our talents. We can let ourselves be while forming ourselves new again.

Writing can help us determine an identity that is true to ourselves and our times. It can help us reinvent ourselves according to what our

"I write because I want more than one life: I insist on a wider selection. It's greed plain and simple."

—*Anne Tyler*

soul wants. No matter how far we have wandered, our spirit can carry us back. Writing awakens our inner connection to everything in the universe. Sometimes you will feel that you are writing in circles toward a sacred place of understanding that nothing is permanent, that everything is changing, and learning to develop a sense of self in that. Trust this process.

"She was the crow of the reservation, she lived off our scraps, and she knew us best because the scraps told our story."

—*Louise Erdrich*

Exercises

1. Choose a concept such as money, work and career, parenting, or independence and write down messages you received about this issue from the important people in your life while you were growing up. How do you live out these messages or rebel against them? What feelings and behaviors would best express who you are today?

2. What do you think you need to develop to have a stronger sense of self and what do you want to cherish as your own? How could you write about your changing and keeping?

DAY 3: SELF-ESTEEM

The better we feel about ourselves, the more able we are to speak up from a sense of self. I once had a young client with a gay father who stopped a homophobic comment among his high school friends. A recent victory on the baseball field had given him the courage to stick up for his father. He kept his tone light and jesting, but he stopped the slur. He said he felt that he was going to faint, but he didn't. He didn't tell his dad what he did, but it made him like his dad more.

I have worked with clients who had lovers or partners who treated them in a way that devalued them without expressing how badly the

"Self-esteem isn't everything; it's just that there's nothing without it."

—*Gloria Steinem*

mistreatment felt. They withheld their feelings, believing either that their value would become apparent in time if they tried hard enough or that they shouldn't be so sensitive to criticism.

Every time we allow someone to treat us as less, we show how little we think of ourselves. We dig ourselves deeper into a trench of internal unhappiness. Through writing, we can gradually release the hurt and begin to fill the trench with rich soil. One client used visualization to fill her trench with straw, but underneath there was a trampoline. She could now feel the hurt and bounce back. She could express herself because she wasn't so affected by past feelings.

"Self-trust, we know, is the first secret of success."

—*Lady Wilde*

Sometimes, when you're feeling bad about yourself, you feel stuck in your writing. You might not want to keep writing about your hurtful relationship or "blue" mood. Carl Jung once said that if you don't understand a dream, try turning it upside down for meaning. Write the opposite of what you are feeling. Perhaps writing what you want and deserve will help you break your sad feelings.

And remember, we do things until we don't need to do them anymore. There's always learning to be had through writing about an experience.

Exercises

1. For ten minutes, write about why it's hard for you to speak freely. Now list the times when you did. What about the situation allowed you to do this? How does speaking up affect your spirit?

2. Just as you might chant for rain, write a chant for better self-love and show this love by expressing your truth. Use this phrase in a repetitive way throughout the chant: I'm moving on. I'm moving on.

DAY 4: BOUNDARIES

There are days when all we need to do to feel good is to sit on a hill overlooking a river and let time slip away watching the boats go by, or days when heaven is lying with us in the tomato patch with a salt shaker. These soulful days show us how much peace we have inside. Our sense of self tells us to relax, to live and enjoy life.

Other times, we must put boundaries on our activities. It is important to begin to realize appropriate boundaries for yourself and others as you develop a better sense of self.

As much as we want to see the last performance of a favorite play before it leaves for another city, it doesn't make sense to stay up late if we have an early work assignment the next day. Or to work late when you've been out for the last three nights and your family needs your love and attention. Or your cold says "Go home."

By choosing one activity we are missing out on another. In our maturity, we know that is all right. What we are looking for is a stimulating yet peaceful life. Freedom is sometimes choosing to do something and sometimes choosing not to, and those choices express our values and who we are.

With practice it becomes easy to set boundaries with those around us. Our spiritual path wants us to set boundaries with kindness. Setting boundaries with others means letting them know by action or words that we can't do what they want, that we need more physical or emotional distance. Boundaries may mean we need to say no. Writing helps us know that when we have drained the well of our body by giving too much away, we cannot be in spirit. The spirit wants you to notice your difference and your doubt and take care of yourself.

It's not rude or unfriendly to set boundaries. It is your right to determine what's comfortable for you. In any relationship, the boundaries need to be mutually decided. Usually people determine what is comfortable for them in informal ways. We sense if someone is a private person and allow them to reveal information about themselves at their own pace. We talk in a softer manner with someone who is gentle; we act boisterous with those who make us laugh. Our culture

"I think knowing what you cannot do is more important than knowing what you can do."
—Lucille Ball

89

tells us how much we can touch another and how close we can stand. Sometimes we need to negotiate with the other person so we can both feel comfortable.

Harvey and Jude met and were immediately comfortable with each other. They both had friendly but unassertive manners. Harvey, however, had trouble with Jude's friend Nadine. Nadine didn't seem to take no for an answer and Harvey felt bombarded with questions. He felt she pushed too hard for her way. He would have to be more assertive if he was going to be around her. In time, he learned that no is a complete sentence. When she asked how much he earned, he asked why she would ask such a question. When she continued to inquire, he said that he didn't discuss his finances with acquaintances.

He was surprised that Nadine didn't seem to mind being told to back off. Instead, she said that people sometimes told her she was a bully and that he should let her know when she made him angry.

The world won't stop spinning if we ask for what we want. It's okay to ask a friend to come over for an hour and help us. It's okay to tell a friend we don't want her to come over even if she's in the neighborhood. We don't owe anyone our poor, tired mind and body. We don't owe anyone our aliveness. It's all right to take a weekend and be with ourselves. To say what we need and don't need. We won't always get our way, but we can express what we want and what makes our spirit happy.

I remember asking my landlord to provide janitorial service for my office. He said he had just been at the office and it looked great. I've learned he always says no to everything at first but that doesn't mean he won't do it. I listened. I didn't try to answer him. I then said what I needed without focusing on his resistance. I listed what chores needed to be done. I asked if the service could start Saturday and he said yes.

When I want to set boundaries over the responsibilities in my life, I often go to water and write. I make lists. I might write ten things I like to do. Then ten things I'd never do. I might ask myself why I don't do them. I look to see what the lists tell me about my life. Am I being playful enough? How can I get recharged? I might use streaming to fantasize what I'd like to take out of my life or bring in.

We are in charge of what we say. Through writing we can get in touch with the soul whose voice wants to bring something golden to our lives. With our growing sense of self, we can live fluidly in the world, doing what is best for our happiness by setting boundaries with love.

"Journal writing is a voyage to the interior."

—Christina Baldwin

Exercises

1. Explore in writing areas in which you may need tighter boundaries: sexually, spiritually, at work, at home, with strangers, with friends. What would you do if your mind was clear and your body relaxed?

2. Think of a boundary issue about which you feel unsure. Ask one of the teachers to dialogue with you and see what the teacher has to say. Now go back and ask all ten teachers to comment. Sometimes we may wonder if we're acting too friendly with a co-worker, for instance. Other times we may realize we have been keeping a distance from a new neighbor and there's no reason not to be friendlier; we were keeping a tight boundary because we were tired.

DAY 5: HONESTY

Alice said she felt as if the world had paused, that her life had spread out before her as she told her boss she couldn't alter the bookkeeping records. He stood staring at her coldly and took the files from her hand without speaking. She went home that night not knowing if she'd have a job in the morning. She would look for work elsewhere, even if he didn't mention the incident. Alice made a tearful call to a friend at another accounting firm for support and resource information. She wrote about the situation until she felt calmer.

"Let your soul do the singin'."

—Ma Rainey

Sometimes, when a situation is dishonest, we have the courage to say no and not participate. Other times we let life take bites out of us. What is important is to find the courage to do what seems right as often as possible. We want the unlit lanterns in our spirits to shine all they can. Honesty brings more light into the world.

We know we have little choice in how we die, but we can decide how we live. A clear sense of self helps us express in honesty what we need to say. Dishonesty is exhausting and drains our life force. Honesty gives us energy.

We breathe more deeply as we watch a witness come forward when a car on a city street is "keyed." We feel better when a friend tells us the reason he hasn't called lately is that he's been turning around financial setbacks and he was stressed. It wasn't anything we had done. Next time he'll try to be vulnerable enough to tell us while the problem is going on so we can be closer.

I've worked with clients who broke their marriage vows. They would tell me they weren't lying but were holding two truths. They loved their wives and they loved their mistresses. I asked them to tell both partners the two truths so that the partners could make a choice for themselves.

We need to know there is honesty of action and words in the world so we can have a place to rest. Honesty creates a sense of safety. Write down lies you are sorry for and let the stars tonight twinkle second chances for you.

"Between the two poles of whole-truth and half-truth is slung the chancy hammock in which we all rock."

—Shana Alexander

Honesty is a balance of behavior and words. The opposite of honesty is not necessarily a lie but an imbalance. The imbalance comes from not knowing ourselves well enough to be able to tell the truth. Honesty is like the layers of an onion. It requires that we keep looking beneath another layer so we can understand ourselves beyond our defenses. We can only be honest after we explore ourselves and our motivations.

Let us work at being kind and honest at the same time. Let's explore through writing what we are projecting and what is the truth. We might pray for deeper understanding. If our intent to be honest has righteousness or anger in it, we recognize this as a triggered emotion and use writing for clarity. By exploring in this way, we can begin to speak honestly with no intent of hurting the other. We speak honestly without meaning to manipulate.

Writing can help us break old family patterns of how we speak to each other when we tell our truth. Remember, without introspection we are like beans on a pole, climbing in the direction we were strung. Why not use your writing to explore and find simpler, kinder ways to express yourself?

Of course, honesty can be elusive. I've had incidents in my life when I thought I was telling the truth only to look back and realize I was in major denial. I've had acquaintances earnestly tell me how they felt and I know they were saying one thing and living another. Were they lying? Was I? Or do we tell the truth as we know it?

I've said I'm sorry when I hurt someone and my apology felt sincere. Later I've realized what I said was honest as far as it went, but I didn't realize how jealousy had played into the situation. Should I go back and say I'm sorry again? Sometimes. Other times I see how human I am in my truth telling.

Rosie was the peacemaker in her family as she was growing up; as an adult, she chose to be with a woman who was more decisive than she. Her partner, Gail, was a direct and assertive woman who was, to Rosie, energetic and exciting. They bought a small home and were furnishing it together. When they shopped, Gail knew immediately what she liked. Rosie was less sure and needed more time to decide, but she let Gail have her way since Gail seemed so sure.

When they got home, Rosie felt resentful. She didn't ask that they take more time to decide because she wasn't clear that's what she needed. She hid her resentment because she didn't think she had the right to feel it. The resentment showed up in other areas of their relationship, such as housekeeping and budgeting.

"I don't tell the truth any more to those who can't make use of it. I tell it mostly to myself, because it always changes me."
—Anaïs Nin

The relationship that was breaking was helped with honest, clear communication. Gail was surprised about Rosie's doubt, but agreed to look for furniture and housewares, go home and think about it, and have Rosie return to make the purchases they had decided on.

Both women started to keep their own journal. On Thursday evenings, they sat down and talked with each other about the concerns of the relationship that week. The set schedule helped Rosie to not feel overwhelmed about having to talk about difficult issues on the spot. She also learned to ask for extra time to respond to a concern if she felt she needed it. The wise women had entered their relationship.

Today they are happy together because they found a way to be honest that worked for them. They now know themselves better. They have a stack of journals and have plans to travel to the Greek islands this summer for their five-year anniversary.

Writing may uncover some buried truths. Revelation and honesty may alter your views about yourself. You may have to deal with traits you'd rather not see. To never misrepresent yourself is to have no place within that is locked, and that is not possible. The goal is to be fierce with your honesty and to be open to feedback. Your writings can point the way to honesty, much like a trusted friend.

Writing can help you deepen your connection to yourself. With a better connection, you can make mistakes and still have good self-esteem to spare. You can know that your sense of self wavers and retreats and comes back to be a friend to you and your soul.

Exercises

1. Write about five situations in which you've observed honesty that you admired. What can you learn from these?

2. What does it mean to you when someone says they hold two truths? How could this represent you at times? How have you expressed this duality?

DAY 6: PRAYER

We can't expand our life awareness to include the spiritual dimension and forget a god force, at least not for long. Even in the dimmest times, we'll have a spiritual sense that something holy is happening. Daily prayer helps keep this knowledge alive.

There are many ways to pray. The wish to pray is a prayer. We can pray with open eyes. We can pray out loud. Whatever we do that asks for guidance outside ourselves is prayer. Prayer is more than meditation. Meditation is seeking the source of strength in one's self. When we pray, we go to a source of strength greater than ourselves.

There is no burden that prayer can't help. When we are not in touch with ourselves, we express our helplessness in prayer. When we don't have the words to form a prayer, we become the prayer. Mother, father, earth can make sense out of confusion even if we cannot. When we are in touch with our sense of self then prayer is a joining. It is a chance to get to know God. With that knowledge we are forever changed. Most of all, prayer changes us so we can change things.

Prayer is an asking for holy courage. Every time we pray we create an energy of calm for ourselves and all who need it. Every time we pray we create more of a sense of self. Anyone who knows how to love knows how to pray. It is an asking, a surrendering, a giving. It is all this at the same time.

Writing can be a form of prayer. Sometimes this is where we must start. After doing everything we can to help an ill friend or calm an injured child, we can write and ask for the spirit's help to live in the delicate storm of flesh. Prayer can tell us to come to beginnings, that death will never bring us to ends. Prayer can fling us into action or quietly take us deeper into the truth of being human.

Wouldn't it be wonderful if, at birth, prayers were offered for

our journey ahead? We would enter the doors of life and all its

"Prayer is a long rope with a strong hold."

—Harriet Beecher Stowe

"The life of a prayer is so great and various there is something in it for everyone. It is like a garden which grows everything, from alpines to potatoes."

—Evelyn Underhill

95

challenges with prayers accompanying us. Any coming anguish would be lessened because we would have the early belief we were not isolated. Our own kind of prayer would be seen as important as food on the table or a wool coat in winter.

At death there would be prayers of gratitude. A thanksgiving for the way we honored our spirit in our lives. A thanksgiving for the way the spirit honored us. Prayer would be seen as a daily practice to keep us in touch with our soul.

"In saying my prayers, I discovered the voice of an innermost self, the raw nerve of my identity."

—*Gelsey Kirkland*

Exercises

1. Write down the different ways you pray and what prayer does for you. How do you pray when the vulture of hate feels trapped within you? How do you pray when sadness squeezes all the lime out of your body? How do you pray when goodness comes your way?

2. Write a prayer that starts with peace for yourself and spreads peace across the sky for all. Write poems as tiny prayers to send into the wind.

DAY 7: REWARDING YOURSELF— MOVEMENT COMES

In this chapter you have been asked to note and develop a stronger sense of self. Take your journal and go out into the world to a vehicle you respond to (a boat, certain car, bike) and describe in vivid language what your vehicle is like. Use metaphors to help you. Write a fantasy of using this vehicle as your transportation to a spiritual place you'd like to go to. Have fun with this and see where it takes you.

WEEK 6: LOVING THE MUSE
THAT TAKES US HOME

Creativity

One of the greatest gifts human beings have been given is the ability to think and act creatively. Perhaps it is the ability to be creative and "see" beyond what is presented that first opened our hearts to our spirits. Or did the spirits open our hearts to creativity?

What we know is that soul and creativity cannot be separated. In Diane di Prima's poem "Rant," she writes that what is most dangerous for us is the death of our imaginations, for imagination is what brings us to wholeness. Imagination allows us to create our lives using memory, dreamwork, and wishes. Imagination gives us creativity every day for ourselves and for the world.

In exploring creativity, we are exploring our soul's desires. Creativity helps us accept our uniqueness as true. When we write a poem or create a visual journal, we feel the flutters of uniqueness moving through us. We touch the heart of our gods when we create. It is a process much like prayer. First we fuss until finally we focus on what is in front of us: fabric, glue, sheets of music, paper, and what is possible. We begin knowing we will be drawn somewhere, though we really don't know where. It's the risk we must take.

There are many ways to strengthen your access to creativity. Just be clever and follow what works for you. Listen to the symphony or take a walk on a wildflower trail if it helps. I love having conversations with Claire Wolf Krantz, a painter who did the cover for my poetry

"Art does not come from thinking but from responding."
—Corita Kent

book, *The Mouth of Home*. Her ideas often set me off on my own ideas for a poem. In one conversation she was talking about immigrants and how they lose their language moving to a new land before they learn the names of birds and flowers. I wrote one of my favorite poems, "No Word for Marigolds," as a direct result of our talk. It says in part, "How would you write your life as story? How would I? If you remember / the place that first held your cry / would it shape your life?" These are questions we might all want to write about.

The title of Anne Lamott's book on writing and life, *Bird by Bird*, is from a time in her life when her brother was struggling to write a report on birds. He was at the kitchen table, close to tears, when their father gave him some good advise, "Bird by bird, buddy. Just take it bird by bird." This is one way we deal with writer's or creative blocks. We just do the next thing.

"Dreams are . . . illustrations from the book your soul is writing about you."
—Marsha Norman

I use my daydreams to create a life truer to the one I want to live. I find that they are a great resource, largely untapped in us. Night dreams also help us know who we are and what our spirit is trying to tell us.

Our creativity asks a muse of new ideas to enter the world. We tap into the well as those before us have done and bring something new to the world.

Day 1: Uniqueness

I remember a quote I once saw in a calendar. It was from Gertrude Stein in *Everybody's Autobiography*, and said, "It takes a lot of time to be a genius, you have to sit around so much doing nothing, really doing nothing." Gertrude, in her writing, was trying to be in the spontaneous creation of writing, thinking, and feeling all at the same time. She used words for their sounds rather than for sense. Her writing style was her way of showing her uniqueness to the world.

"The best thing about being God would be the making of the heads."
—Iris Murdoch

Coming from a family where sitting and doing nothing was punishable by tasks in the kitchen or yard, I responded to the idea of sitting doing nothing but being a genius. My friend Bonnie and I have recently implemented this as a ritual when we get together after a hard day at the office, before our swim and creative work. We lie down on the couches of my living room to practice our genius for a while. I have to say, it makes us unique if not strange . . . and we like this.

I have many clients who worry about not being unique enough. This is a cousin to not being good enough, not being successful. It comes from society's insistent voice of who's on first and who's on second. This competition, internalized in our minds, does not help us and must be coaxed to rest. We are what we are. We assess as we can. As you let yourself relax into creativity, pay attention to the wonderful feelings and life you have. It's first and foremost for you to enjoy. A nurse friend says doing her patchwork quilt in the evenings is her heaven. She also says my garden is a piece of heaven. She may not notice it, but heaven is a great deal in her life because she is spirit and service and creativity.

Our uniqueness gives our authentic self a voice. We can start by keeping a journal and using writing as spiritual practice. Rosemary Ruether in *Sexism and God-Talk* writes: "[The] liberating encounter with the God/ess is always an encounter with our authentic selves resurrected from underneath the alienated self. It is not experienced against, but in and through relationships, healing our broken relations with our bodies, with other people, with nature." I would add with art and creativity.

> *"Genius is the gold in the mine, talent is the miner who works and brings it out."*
> —Lady Marguerite Blessington

> *"Nothing is repeated and everything is unparalleled."*
> —Emond and Jules de Concourt

Exercises

1. We are often teased about or criticized for a quality that is seen as a weakness but is actually a strength. This strength may lead to our uniqueness. For instance, a sensitive person might become a gifted intuitive leader. Do *listmaking* to clarify the ways this has happened to you.

2. Think of someone from your life, reading, or film who could be your role model based on their acceptance of their own uniqueness. What is their uniqueness? What is yours? Write about this in your journal.

3. What would you call a book on uniqueness? What would the chapters be titled? What ideas would the book share with the readers?

DAY 2: RISK-TAKING

"Creation lives alone in a small temple. Only one may worship at a time."

—*Nancy Hale*

"When we are writing, or painting, or composing, we are, during the time of creativity, freed from normal restrictions, and are opened to a wider world, where colors are brighter, sounds clearer, and people more wonderously complex than we normally realize."

—*Madeleine L'Engle*

As we come to appreciate our uniqueness, the world loosens its grip on us. Some cleverer self emerges. Words pour out across the page and we can feel them sliding out from a place beyond self-consciousness. We read what we have written and it's "one silver midnight the moon was full of tiny stars waiting to break off to form souls." We can feel our hearts open. We know those words were written by our fingers, but we also know a force helped us. We find ourselves relaxing into the feeling that all is well. So much is given to us and we receive our gift of creativity with a joy and satisfaction that enlivens and enriches life. And brings faith. We sit with the feeling that life is as good as it gets right at this moment. Gratitude, we feel a heavenly gratitude for life on earth in our body.

Often, we happily start a creative project, and then comes the time of anxiety. The anxiety needs to happen. Call it excitement of a new place where we don't know who or where we are. Hang in and don't back out and get through the wanderland by reaching something that feels "right." It might be a direction for a book, a line in a poem that sums it up or opens it up, a movement that propels the dance forward, a color space adding variance to a painting. With this comes the calm and the expansion of spirit.

This "wanderland" can be exhilarating, a place that we long for, or a dangerous place where addictions can enter. Drinking or drugs may help reduce the anxiety or excitement, but it will also give you a new problem, one that will drain your spirit. Hang on for the ride, know that you're supposed to feel uncertain for a while, and the new life will form. The "wanderland" just might be the time when your spirit is finding your soul.

Before one of my clients begins her creative work, she sits down and has an imaginary talk with her father, who dreads taking risks. She also talks to the armadillo she's carried with her all her life that holds her fear. She then lets them stay in her comfortable living room while she goes to her studio and uses the affirmation "This is good." This ritual helps keep dread and fear in the living room and allows her to get on to her sculpting.

By setting up a life that is more in keeping with your spirit, you risk displeasing others. Sometimes, you risk your ability to support yourself. Through writing and speaking to your wise self, you can explore what is best for you and do it. You must keep in mind that you must be in balance between the practical world and the creative and spiritual world and find a way to make it work. Risky, yes. Rewarding, yes, yes, yes. By writing in your journal you can see if you can lean toward living the life that would energize your spirit.

Virginia Woolf once wrote, "When I ask you to write more books I am urging you to do what will be for your good and for the good of the world at large." Every time someone models a way to find time for their creativity, they show us how to live. Every time someone shares a struggle, he or she is saying that this is what counts and I'm trying to learn how to live it. We can help each other by taking risks and sharing.

Creativity is not all smooth sailing, but it's worth doing because it teaches us a truth about ourselves and the world. "Now I accept that facing the difficult is part of the heroic journey of writing. A preparation, a ritual of sanctification that it is through this arduous process of grappling with words that writing becomes my true home, a place of solace and comfort," says the black essayist bell hooks.

Writing in your journal you learn what has been inside your mind, heart, and imagination for such a long time. You may also explore other art forms, always asking: What do I love?

"Sometimes I wonder what the difference is between being cautious and being dead."
—*Sue Grafton*

Exercises

1. Write down the important authority figures of your childhood. What was their relationship to risk? How are you like that or not like that? Write an affirmation for each part of yourself that might be like that. If mom was cautious, you might say to this part of yourself, "I'm independent. I can decide."

2. When have you seen risk in a movie or read about a character in a book taking a risk and admired that action? Is there a place in your life where you could make it your own behavior?

3. Do *dialoguing* with Mr. or Mrs. Risk and learn the first steps to overcoming barriers.

DAY 3: REDUCING BLOCKS

When I can't seem to write, I go out and buy new reams of paper and toner, alphabetize my notes, file my papers, and do research to find quotations or new ideas. When it's difficult to write I do the business end of writing and publishing. And, of course, I moan to my friends and read famous quotations and listen to sounds from the world and look for messages. And pray! And journal or doodle. I trust that the juice will come back!

This afternoon I felt too scattered to write, so I went to a tiny neighborhood bookstore, Mama Bear's, and found a book called *The Woman Who Spilled Words All Over Herself* by Rosemary Daniels. She says, "We don't have to be perfect people, or healthy people to write." Thank goodness, I thought.

She talks about self-sabotage, or how good writers shoot themselves in the foot. Daniels lists lack of self-discipline, failure to use time positively, failing to finish, not honoring one's own unique material, and failing to analyze one's own process and strengths, among our foot-shooting-faults. Go through this list and write how these might or might not be true for you. Take a look at your foot.

"I do not want to die . . . until I have faithfully made the most of my talent and cultivated
 the seed that was placed in me until the last small twig has grown."
—*Kathe Kollwitz*

I received an e-mail the other day from a writer friend, Lonnie Hull

Dupont, that said, "Be faithful to your talent." That message came at

a time when I was lacking in courage. I realized that if I went back

to the fun of writing using any talent I had, I could start again.

So many times clients come to me wanting to use hypnotherapy to release artistic blocks. Sometimes they need to envision the story or dance and go and do it. Others have needed a kind angel on their shoulder to encourage them. Others needed to let go of old negative voices that they still carry with them. Here are some of the most common obstacles and the solutions we've come up with. I've used writing but it could be any art form.

Problem	Solutions
I don't write well enough.	Dare to be average.
	Do what you can.
	Be playful with your writing.
	Read cartoons. Write jokes.

Problem	Solutions
I don't have time.	Make your talent a priority. No more favors to others until you've accomplished your promise to yourself. Use a cat for a picture of self-care.
I must succeed.	Do what you love and like it. Dare to fail. There's no chance to achieve if you don't try. Use the image of a cup of gold coins or of an energetic bubbling brook.
I am depressed.	Write because you may find another life (aliveness) in your creativity. Feel the spirit in the wind calling to you.
I don't know enough.	So what do you know?! Be the boss! No more research. Do it and have a friend check in on you for support.
I can't get organized.	Ring a bell. This signals time to prepare and begin. When thoughts get muddled or anxiety comes, ring the bell again.
Writing gets boring.	Imagine the fun of a book reading.
I have too much energy to sit and write.	Write at work on your lunch hour or break.
It's hard for me to focus.	Write down what you are writing in an easy-to-read structure and follow it. Use large chart paper.

One of the things I have learned from working with clients both in trance and with writing is that the subconscious is always trying to protect us. Maybe the subconscious is on the wrong track and the protection is outdated. The dancer who can't perform because she'll be humiliated can coax the subconscious to see the reality of today. She has taken her lessons. She has learned her craft. She has skill. The critical authority figure of the past will not be invited and even if he shows up, today is not yesterday. She can find a new body sensation instead of humiliation and practice performing with that sensation.

Writer Anne Lamott feels that when we say we're blocked, we're really empty, and that we need to accept this. She has her students "write one page of anything, three hundred words of memories or dreams or stream of consciousness or how much they hate writing— just for the hell of it, just to keep their fingers from becoming too arthritic . . ." It's like calling in your spirit and asking the spirit to be honest. You can grumble. You can be real. Lamott reminds us that writing can soothe us. Or as she mentions in a quote by Marianne Moore, "The world's an orphan's home," and we can give ourselves and others the gift of connection through our art. When we create, we are re-creating ourselves.

"Storytelling reveals meaning without committing the error of defining it."

—Hannah Arendt

Exercises

1. How have you experienced times when nothing creative happened? No garden. No cooking. No writing. Just the mundane of life happening over and over. Write where the mundane leads. Now write how you got out of this blocked time. What was it about, really? What do you need to remind yourself if you find yourself blocked again?

2. Using listmaking, write down favorite childhood books or fairy tales. If you liked *The Little Lame Prince*, how did you feel crippled and how could this be a block? How have you overcome or not

overcome this feeling? If you liked *The Secret Garden*, how did you or didn't you create a secret life? How can these be blocks and how can they be undone? Explore in streaming and then write down some affirmations that you can tape up on your refrigerator, such as "I move freely." "I can do what I want." Or "I have a beautiful garden within me."

3. Using *gazing into the waters*, imagine a stream blocked until the rains come and wash away debris. Let your body feel the freeing and use this as an image metaphor for unblocking.

DAY 4: STRENGTHENING ACCESS TO CREATIVITY

Pearl Buck was once quoted in the *New York Post* saying that "Inside myself is a place where I live all alone and that's where you renew your springs that never dry out." The place where you are most creative is the place where you can be the happiest. It can also be a place of great loneliness as we cast about in exploration before the light or words come. Creativity makes days both lonely and balmy. Choose it if you want the feeling of being alive even when it hurts, find an outlet to express the feelings alive in your life right now.

For me, inspiration is my access. I don't wait for it to come. I go to wherever it is for me in that moment. I listen to music, I walk in nature, I read poetry, I read famous quotations before turning out the light and going to sleep. I might write a line and I know it's the first line of a poem. I hear a conversation on the bus and I write a take on it. I use my life as inspiration for creativity.

I was telling a friend that I dreamt a poem's first line: "I killed my father and ate his trout." I wanted to explore the meaning of this. She said she'd have to sleep more so she could hear poems. We laughed and she said that, actually, she'd never heard poems, but if she got a decent night's sleep, she might have the energy to take up modern dance again.

Remember things you loved when you were a child and see if there are clues. Ask your friends. An acupuncturist friend once asked for feedback on what I thought her talent might be beyond healing. "Dialogue," I said, "and performance," for I remembered how, after a poetry reading, she told us a story of a surgeon in Ireland, Mr. Hodges. I don't remember the story, but I remember our laughter and her accent. Occasionally, a friend will call and ask for Mr. Hodges and we'll start laughing again. Use your friends, ask for their opinion.

The clues are in your life. My mother loves color and, after thirty-two years of working in the home, took a job selling draperies. She loved working with color and fabric. When I asked her how she decided what to do, she said she knew she wanted to work with homemakers and she wrote out lists of what she could offer them. She didn't care enough about the right scarf or pin, but the large sweep of color over the window was of interest to her. And her interest in art's weave and texture helped.

"What I have found is, anything one keeps hidden should now and then be hidden somewhere else."
—Elizabeth Bowen

Other people have other ways of accessing creativity. I know a woman who finds her creativity when she feels playful and writes country-western songs reminding her of her years in Tennessee. Some like to be productive and efficient and develop the latest gadget or the best high-rise. Others may create from feelings, some from ideas. A friend of mine works on her novel every morning from eight to noon—a very well developed structure. Some like working to deadlines made by others or themselves. A cartoonist friend knows the idea he is going to draw a cartoon on but waits until he's done many sketches before he decides which to use. A neighbor learns about himself from travel and uses the colors and designs from the world to "seed" his fabric designs.

People invent because they are tinkerers. They sing because they were given a talent that makes them feel confident. Mozart composed because he heard music playing in his head: it was fun. Some like to sculpt in public places because it helps them feel large and in control. Other artists look for peace by working with pastels.

If you decide to put together a writing group or join one, be sure that it offers support, stimulation, and that the members are expected to be committed to their writing and take it seriously. You want the concentration on your strengths; when you trust the others and know their work, you know where they are coming from, you can accept respectful comments on your weaknesses. Remember, you will not be doing yourself any favors if you allow another critical judge in your life.

The muse is excited and expanded by stimulation. When I hear Carolyn Forche read her poems I am not envious, I am elated. When I read Linda Hogan I am transported and my muse says yes to writing. You want to feel this kind of stimulation in any writing group; just being glad to hear their ideas and what they have written can help your writing. Greatness encourages your writing while mediocre works make you tired.

If you have no writing group or yours is taking a summer break, read your work into a tape recorder. Listen to it the next day; sometimes you'll hear that what you have said isn't as clear as you thought. Sometimes you'll notice magic in the sound and rhythm of words. It's like taking the time to reread what you've written the next day.

There are activities and people you may have to give up when you write. We prioritize. When I was writing my first poetry book I tried to keep up with everything I'd been doing and write the book, too. All it did was make me frustrated. I felt much less overwhelmed when I cut back on my teaching and social schedule and gave myself the time I needed. I am willing to sacrifice to write, but not to the extent that I feel isolated or resentful.

Start getting poetry anthologies from the library. You can read several poems each day, and besides getting educated, you'll fuel your imagination. Poetry asks you to be in touch with your senses and with the details of life. I wrote the line: "the turning of the Ferris wheel, so high you might catch what you want." Then I explored that further in my writing and realized I wanted to see beyond the narrow window I had set up for my life at the time.

I have been talking about feeding the muse. By loving some of the same things each year and different things some years, we feed the muse. By learning to live well by listening, doing, reflecting, observing, and reading, you are in a life state to replenish yourself. If your life is good, you will have many thoughts, feelings, and actions to write about.

I recently picked up a book of essays by bell hooks, *Remembered Rapture*. Reading an essay is an excellent way to stimulate your mind and can give you much material to write about. Hooks talks about writing from a place of suffering: "I knew when I sat at the feet of Miss Zula, who could barely move because illness had caused her dark body to grow huge and monstrous, reading letting my tongue and breath caress written words, giving voice to passions she would never know I knew then I wanted a life in words. I wanted to be a writer. I wanted to be able to enter this sacred realm at will and find there the meaning of grace."

Exercises

1. Take four magazines and choose pictures you do and don't connect to. On one side of a piece of cardboard glue the pictures to which you connect. On the other, glue the pictures to which you don't connect. Do some *streaming* or *dialoging* for insight. Pretend you have to hold up your collages and give a presentation entitled "Accessing My Creativity." Write down what the collages tell you about your soul and creative life.

2. Write to a young person and tell him what is most important about life and how creativity fits into this. What does your advice tell you about your life?

3. Who would you want to see or spend an hour with? Why that person? What does it tell you about yourself and your creativity?

Day 5: Using Day and Night Dreams

"If you pay attention to your dreams, they will begin to speak to you."

—Natalie Goldberg

Another way to access our creativity is through our dreams. What we daydream has clues and signals about what we want and need. Night dreaming can help you better understand yourself and your shadow life. Night dreaming often shows what we are working through in our lives.

I wasn't brought up in a time where people used visualization. I was never asked to create an image or energy feeling of what I wanted. I wouldn't have been able to actualize my life through visualizing because I would have hoped too small. If I had any hope at all it would have been to cope and not be anxious. I wanted to be normal or not normal, I wasn't sure. But from the earliest age, I daydreamed. I put myself in a garden I liked and relaxed there. I practiced conversations where I stuck up for myself. I practiced conversations where I had to tell someone something difficult. I daydreamed what I would do if I were rejected in Brownies. What if I failed? I daydreamed about how I'd like to feel and what I'd like to have happen. I'd set up a scenario of being given money. I'd practice how gracious I'd be. How lovingly I'd spend the money. I would daydream exactly how much I would give to each person. I'd have my own spending plan.

My daydreaming prepared me for life and it certainly helped create me as a hypnotherapist, writer, and teacher.

Night dreams have a life of their own. They might explore conflicts you are dealing with in your waking life. Ten years after my divorce I dreamt that I had decided not to leave my husband. In the dream I hadn't told him that I wouldn't be having sex with him, and that worried me some. I knew that the dream was a way of working through ambiguities. When I awoke, I wrote down my feelings and realized the dream was a signal that life was feeling too hard. It was time for me to take time off and play.

"A dream—you know—is a mind that looks over the edge of things."

—Mary O'Hara

A client once came to me upset by a dream she kept having in which she had to get rid of her family pictures. The dream said throw the pictures away. Her husband and children didn't want her to throw away their albums. She didn't really want to either. However, the thought wouldn't go away. After exploring and doing some writing on this, she felt the message was to throw away the pictures of the early years of her marriage that were in her mind. She had been unhappy as a young wife and mother. In the last years, her husband had been more understanding and kind and now they were close. She was happier as a mom as the children got older. She needed to bring her attention into the present and to release the past. Her thoughts when she dreamed were trying to tell her something but she needed help in decoding the message.

Dreams of the stories the subconscious mind tells about ourselves sometimes use the language of story, myth, and symbols. Some dreams help us see the great spirit in our life. Sometimes mother-father-spirit talks to us. It's helpful to keep a dream section in your journal and to write down your dreams before they and their message slip away from you.

> "During the day, our souls gather their impressions of us, how our lives feel. . . . Our spirits collect these impressions, keep them together, like wisps of smoke in a bag. Then, when we're asleep, our brains open up these bags of smoke . . . and take a look."
>
> —Marsha Norman

Exercises

1. Close your eyes and go back into a dream. Recount it. Do the following Dream Sourcing exercise.

   Dream Sourcing
   1. Write down a dream.
   2. Choose the main feelings in the dream.
   3. Choose the main images.
   4. Decide in a sentence or two what the dream is about.
   5. Give the dream a title.

6. Decide the question the dream asks.
7. Do wise speaking dialogues with the main images/people of the dream.
8. Ask each image/person for a gift.
9. Tell the meaning of the dream. Or reverse the meaning of the dream.

2. Think of a recent dream and try using this *Coming Together* technique to help you decipher it:

Coming Together
1. Write down your dream.
2. List the main players in the dream. They could be a neighbor, a cat, an ice cream cone, a friend, your sister or brother.
3. List the actions of the main players. For instance, the neighbor retreating from a cat's hissing, a cat hissing.
4. Write down how each of the main players is a part of you.
5. Acknowledge all parts of yourself and, using *gazing into the waters*, ask the dream what it wants you to know. You may want to then ask how your parts can work in harmony since they are all a part of you. You might, for example, decide the part of you that is afraid must learn from the hissing part how to defend you.

3. What dream would you like to make happen? Ask the dream to join your life. Use *clustering* and *streaming*.

DAY 6: COMMITMENT

Commitment is about freely giving in trust. We entrust ourselves with a task to see the purple light at dusk filled with the brush of the spirit. We are not imprisoned. We chose to fulfill this wish to ourselves.

In *The Journals and Letters of the Little Locksmith* there is a quote by Katharine Butler Hathaway that I used years ago on a holiday card. It reads: "Then and there I invented this rule for myself to be applied to every decision I might make in the future. I would sort out all the arguments and see which one belonged to fear and which to creativeness and other things being equal, I would make the decision which had the larger number of creative reasons on its side. I think it must be a rule something like this that makes jonquils and crocuses come pushing through the cold mud."

"Most new discoveries are suddenly seen things that were always there."

—*Susanne K. Langer*

This is the kind of commitment my friends who seem to derive the most pleasure out of their creative work have. They have chosen the long hours and the work. They have chosen to be alone in their studios. They learn how to collage together a life with enough money and enough energy and time. They know some seasons, some years are better than others. They live a practical and creative life and talk about living in two worlds. They feel their spirit by doing their creative work. They do what it takes to make this happen and record their creative process in their journals to serve as a reminder in the future. They aren't victims but rather they choose creativity to bring their spirit to their life. Creating makes them happy.

Sometimes we don't keep our commitments to ourselves because they aren't the right choice. I remember setting up a darkroom in my garage, taking classes, buying equipment, taking an extra job on a local newspaper as an "on call" reporter, and putting together a portfolio of black-and-white fine-art prints. I had a one-woman show in a gallery and I loved the experience. However, once the show was over, I didn't want to go back into the darkroom. I remembered the excitement of finding the image in the world or staging it, choosing the image from the roll, and watching the image come up in the pan. But I still didn't want to start in again.

I gave myself a break and wrote for a while. I discovered that I had been grasping at straws when I set out on a photography career and that I really didn't like the technical end. I didn't like the chemicals. I hated being alone so much in the dark. I'm much happier writing at my window watching my star jasmine grow, noting the hummingbirds hunt and decide which of my flowers to derive nourishment from today.

I'm not sorry I spent those years on photography. I have some great prints on my walls and I have given many to others. It's fun to know a lot of an art and to appreciate it in the everyday and in museums. I love taking pictures, and to this day I know I have an eye and use it in the balance of the images. Still, it was the wrong commitment to continue any longer. Maybe using photography as a graphic line was pure poetry and my entranceway. All I knew is that I needed to commit to something more in the light of day.

Exercises

1. Remember a time when you wanted something but you didn't get it. Write about that experience. Now write about a time when you wanted something and you got it. What was the difference?

2. Going back to exercise one, how can you bring what you didn't get back into your life, perhaps in an altered form?

3. On a piece of lovely paper, write the commitment you have to yourself. Write how much it means to you. Write what you are willing to do. Share with one loyal person when you are ready.

DAY 7: REWARDING YOURSELF—
FOLLOWING THE PULSE

This week we have been talking about opening our spirits so we can find our creativity. Today, as your reward, go out into the world and find a place that can be your muse for creativity. You may not find the right place the first time you look, so seek out a place near your home as a start. This place should make you feel alive in your creativity. Is it filled with action and people so your creative juice can run? Is it a place of quiet where moss can spread? Once you find your place, write down why it is right for you. You might try writing a commitment to this place or a prayer about it and what it could mean in your life. How can the muse tap and choose you here?

WEEK 7: THE PATH WITH A HEART

Integration

In Mexico there is a saying, *"La vida es corta, pero ancha."* Life is short, but it's wide. We have the time to bring together what makes us feel whole. First we must notice what we value. Our wise person teaches us that we need love and friendship to keep us happy and healthy, and work and creativity to allow us to be self-sufficient and fulfilled. We must pay attention to our bodies, our sexuality, our spirituality, and our need for solitude.

Some people rebel against the idea that they have to make up their mind and instead live lives that show what they value: a life of family and children, a life of career and city stimulation, a life of geography and quiet hills. This can work, but too often we don't get the chance to experience the life we would really like to live, and so life is spent with little of what we love.

How much richer and fuller our lives would be if we could integrate some of what we love into all of life's stages. It can help if you make a practice of writing down the things you love. I always try to make a record when I do something I love. I use my writing to reevaluate how I spend my time. I write down the things I think I want to do and then ask myself if I really want to do them. If I do, I move on with it and make a plan. What would be the first steps to doing what I want? If I realize that this is not something I want to do, I am content. It doesn't fester.

In *The Teachings of Don Juan,* Carlos Castaneda poses the following question: "Before you embark on [a new path], ask the question: Does this path have a heart? If the answer is no, you will know it, and then you must choose another path. . . . A path without a heart is never enjoyable. You have to work hard even to take it. On the other hand, a path with a heart is easy; it does not make you work at liking it."

"Spiritual love is a position of standing with one hand extended into the universe and one hand extended into the world, letting ourselves be a conduit for passing energy."

—Christina Baldwin

A client, Bet, said her life changed when she realized she could have people live her life with her. Some family, a friend from long ago, a friend who shared her spiritual seeking, a friend to tell secrets to. Coming from her family, she never thought about sharing her lifetime with anyone unless she found "a soul mate." She was already in a good partnership, but now she was developing a further understanding of community. Now, when her daughter felt burdened by a request from her mother, the daughter could say no and count on others on her mother's team to pitch in.

Bet described to me the relief on her daughter's face when she realized there were others who could be counted on to help her mother. Because this expanded community was still such a new concept to Bet, she understood her daughter's relief. Building the kind of community she wanted gave her *and* her daughter a chance for a better relationship and life.

We can use our journal to ask the wise person to help us to not desert our own form of talent. "Some people are born to lift heavy weights, some are born to juggle golden balls," says the critic Max Beerbohm. Choose to do your work the best you can with a soft heart and a great spirit. Set a goal to find out what work would make you happy and carry it out. "Work and play are words to describe the same thing under differing conditions," says Mark Twain. Perhaps you know what this feels like. Set any goals and write out what they are and who will do what by when.

"Few are the giants of the soul who actually feel that the human race is their family circle."

—Elizabeth Wray Taylor

Remember, powerful people trust their instincts. We just have to turn that power to our personal life and include the integration of what we value.

Starhawk writes in *Truth and Dare*, "Spirituality promotes passivity when the domain of spirit is defined as outside the world. When this world is the terrain of spirit, we ourselves become actors in the story, and this world becomes the realm in which the sacred must be honored and freedom created." This is the integration we are seeking.

As we integrate the important areas of our lives we must also take a look at solitude. Colette writes, "There are days when solitude, for some my age, is a heady wine that intoxicates you with freedom, others when it is a bitter tonic, and still others when it is a poison that makes you beat your head against the wall." So we need to find how solitude can serve us and how we can serve solitude. We need to try to get to that place Tillie Olsen writes about in *Tell Me a Riddle* when she says, "She would not exchange her solitude for anything. Never again to be forced to move to the rhythms of others."

*"We never touch
but at points."*
—Ralph Waldo Emerson

DAY 1: LOVE

Creating a life rooted in love is one of the greatest challenges and joys on the spiritual path. Know *yourself* and you will be better prepared for love and its heights. "Use writing to help you see your confusion and bring your challenges down to a conquerable size," says Victoria Moran in *Creating a Charmed Life*. "It is an invaluable aid in creating a charmed life. It can also help you from losing your temper or sinking into self-pity." She keeps her journal in her nightstand next to the flashlight and uses it for the same reason: extra light.

Mozart felt that love was the soul of genius. When we love, the muse is flying at our shoulder like Peter Pan's Tinkerbell asking us to let the ocean's waves, the white noise, come closer. We are vulnerable and can examine the creative edge and find something new. "To love deeply in one direction makes us more loving in all others," says Anne-Sophie Swetchine in *The Writings of Madame Swetchine*. "Love has the quality of informing almost everything—even one's work," says New Zealand writer and educator Sylvia Ashton-Warner.

*"Writing, which is my
form of celebration
and prayer, is also
my way of inquiry."*
—Diane Ackerman

I have a client who loves to sing and got a gig at a jazz club in Atlanta. She was more involved in her singing and the business of music than she had been in years, and then in walks the man of her dreams. She wasn't looking for love. She "didn't have the time" or "the energy" to fall in love, but that didn't matter. This man, a collector of seventeenth-century music scores and a great music lover, was attracted to her love of music and the energy that followed her everywhere because of this love. Love blossomed because she was already living in love. They've been together for seven years.

No matter who you are or where you are in your life, there is always something left to love.

If you feel as if there is no starting place for you today, go to a park and watch the children. Watch the dogs bring back their sticks. Children and animals have love to give and show it. Sometimes all you need to do is to open your heart to the possibility of love and you will find sweet cherries and plums on your table to nurture you back to your spirit, where love resides.

"Love is a context, not a behavior." —*Marilyn Ferguson*

Exercises

1. Write down the times you have been in love in your lifetime. What were the lessons of that love? Notice if you've had a love that helped you to develop yourself. What was developed and how did the relationship help? You may want to explore the opposite and write how love relationships have taken you away from yourself. What were the signals that your self was being lost? Was there room in the relationship to do things differently? What are the lessons here?

2. Write to a young person in your life and tell him or her what is the most important thing to remember about love. You can keep the letter in your journal or ask if the youngster would like to see it.

3. Write on your ambivalence about love and how that affects your love life. Now write about a miracle in you.

4. Write about the ways in which you love yourself.

"After ecstasy, the laundry." —Zen saying

DAY 2: FRIENDSHIPS AND FAMILY

So many times after being with a friend I think of Emily Dickinson's line: "It gives me shelter to talk to you." On this second day of our exploration of integration, I'm hoping we can begin to use our journals as our shelter and our friend.

I didn't learn the importance of friendship from my family, but other women were there to teach me. I learned to give back. If you didn't feel loved as a child, you might be surprised when a friend shows his or her love for you by going to a doctor's appointment with you or by telling you the hard things you need to hear to keep you on the right path.

"Friendship is the bread of the heart."
—Mary Russell Mitford

Friendship also helps to heal the past. We can love someone like a brother who we never got to love. We can be close to our partner in a way we wanted to be close to our original family. Women friends can be the sisters we always wanted. Friends can also help us relieve guilt and dissolve anger. All our lives we've been trying to be close to someone, and this time we're successful.

One of the rewards of having friendships with siblings and family members is the shared history. As we struggle to understand our ambivalent and sometimes contradictory feelings toward our kin, we have someone of whom we can ask, "Remember when . . .?"

"Call it a clan, call it a network, call it a tribe, call it a family. Whatever you call it, whoever you are, you need one."
—Jane Howard

Most of us have roles assigned to us in our families. These roles may have very little to do with who we are. Sometimes a friend within the family can validate that for us. She may have history that she can share with us that explains how we got that role or how she saw that it didn't fit. The uncle of my friend Nancy told her that her mother was still grieving the loss of her father when she was born. He talked in detail about that year. Knowing that her mother had taken long walks at night while she slept in her crib validated Nancy's sense that her mother had been there but not there. This helped Nancy explore at a deeper level what she had always felt—abandoned—and why she had trouble with attachment. She used her writing practice to dialogue with her absent mother, her grandfather's spirit, and the youngster she once was, and found that her spirit could be with her in this new knowledge.

Many times in friendship, however, we are seen as we *were* and not as we are. It's important to reveal who we have become and who we are becoming. Family members and old friends may remind us of the parts of ourselves that we have left behind. Yet they are in our lives because they represent a time of our life that still has meaning for us. It might help to write about your friends and see what time of your life they represent and how that's important to you. And you can always try updating them. Sometimes we change and forget to tell others.

Our friendships sometimes mirror our fantasies. I have a client whose boyfriend is a dancer and she always wanted to use her body more and be in better shape. His energetic life encourages her. Others admire in a friend the free spirit of travel or the steadiness of work loved.

It's important to evaluate ourselves as friends from time to time. Who have we been taking for granted? Who needs a minute of our time? Who would appreciate a card talking about their wise spirit and how you appreciate that quality in them? We can promise ourselves to be better friends. Promise yourself to ask a question after a friend talks rather than to comment. Not busying yourself formulating a response might help you really listen.

Friendship, whether inside the family or in a family of our own making, helps us integrate the past with support and learnings in the present. If we're lucky and take care, we can take these loved ones to our future and continue to share all that we are.

Exercises

1. Write down the times you have felt a spiritual connection with a friend. What brings this sense out in you? Give examples. Write about the fantasy friends in your life and what they represent. Also notice to whom you respond in books and movies. Write what that says about you.

2. Ask a friend to tell you what she likes best about you. Ask this friend to give you some comments on what you need to do. Use *streaming* to explore what it was like to ask and on the comments you received.

3. Tell someone what knowing them has meant to you.

4. List your friends and how you find yourself in them.

DAY 3: WORK AND CREATIVITY

Two of the hardest things to integrate are spirit and work. We often wonder how we can work from eight to five and still be in touch with our creativity. How can we work in corporate America with a growing sense of self and our own uniqueness? What can we bring to the culture and how can the culture change to help us on this path? How can creativity be used in a day-to-day job or at least not be snuffed out? How can thinking creatively help us be better people and better employees?

I've listened to many clients over the years as they survive high-pressured, responsible jobs. Some love their work and thrive on the pressure and feeling of accomplishment. But they usually have to be reminded not to crash and burn. These people need to learn relaxation techniques and how to put personal goals into their work schedule. Relaxation, like anything else, can be an accomplishment. I once asked a top manager to keep a journal on her fear of failure. She said

"Imagine what a harmonious world it could be if every single person, both young and old, shared a little of what they are good at doing."

—Quincy Jones

she didn't want to waste the time, but she did it anyway. Gradually she realized she was loved for what she did and not for who she was. Next she wrote on "being" rather than "doing," and how that might look in a healthy balance. Her boyfriend was delighted with the change in her. Through her writing, she saw glimmers of work and self in concert.

Some folks just like their work and aren't interested in climbing the ladder. I have a client who was looked down on for passing up promotions, but she was content with her responsibilities at the large company where she worked. She wanted time for her music and her friends and family. She commands a good salary, has a few allies, and works in a humane way with new hires and those needing help with their benefits (her job). She isn't as appreciated for her work as she could be, but she focuses on taking care of herself and the employees she helps. She enjoys devising new systems that better work for the employees, and changes orientations regularly as she notices what seems to be understood and what seems to be confusing. She hates office politics and views her interactions with others as her boundary lessons and uses them to grow. She considers work a spiritual practice; it's a hard practice but she feels her growth. She finds a way to make her work work for her.

> "Sometimes you win, sometimes you lose, sometimes you get rained out."
>
> —Satchel Paige

To be in corporate America and be honest and fair helps others. To be someone to be counted on to act kindly counts. You can be the heart of a place in a toxic work situation if you can bear it. You can do the same work with a less toxic boss if you care to move to another company. With a plan, you can change your career. You decide if it would be better for you to have a job and not a career. It helps to know you have choices even when it doesn't feel as if you do. Listen to others and their stories. Start to think in a more optional way.

Sometimes it helps to write out your situation from three different perspectives. These may be from your optimistic self, your stuck self, and your practical self. Or it could be the view from yourself, your boss, and your co-worker. Writing from varying points of view helps you to open your small window. You may be surprised at what you come up with.

My experience is that people with high motivation and drive can make the necessary changes because they believe they can; they can make the commitment and are willing to work to make it happen. I know a secretary who became a computer trainer, a graphic artist who became a minister, a minister who is now an accounts manager and spends his money on art. Or, you can stay where you are, decide it is good enough, and change yourself to make it work for you spiritually and creatively.

"I like work,
it fascinates me.
I can sit and look
at it for hours."
—Jerome K. Jerome

More and more people are exploring questions of creativity and spirituality on the job and in writing. That's a start. You may find a co-worker who can keep you grounded in these issues, someone with whom you can talk about issues beyond the actual work and office politics. How can you help each other stay sane with all the pressure and nonsense. Who are your allies? How can you do the right thing? What are you learning?

"Let not what you cannot do tear from your hand what you can."—Ashanti proverb

You can use this book and the exercises to learn more about yourself and your contributions. You can journal what you want to have accomplished at the end of your life if you never left this job and the creative qualities you used to accomplish these goals.

You can have clearly defined artistic goals for your after-work hours. It is difficult to go to your studio after a long day, and defined goals help. Natalie goes to the studio in her garage on Wednesday evenings and all day Sunday. These are her creative hours, and she views them as sacred. Saturday she does errands and goes out with her partner. Monday, Tuesday, Thursday, and Friday nights she cleans her house for thirty minutes and rests by reading. She socializes mostly at work with those she finds creative and spiritual. Her art this year is making huge and wonderful mud bears. She has three weeks vacation and spends one week at home loafing, one week in her studio, and one week seeing something she hasn't seen before: Mono Lake, Grand

Canyon, the quaint town of Port Townsend. Natalie says she doesn't need to go far and see another world. Her other world is in her garage.

The important thing is to begin to operate in the truth: where you go, there you are. That means, you exercise your spiritual muscle wherever you are. You don't drive every activity. You are patient. You trust others when you can. You ask for help. You take your spiritual and creative self wherever you go and so it begins to matter less where you are.

Richard N. Bolles, the author of *The Three Boxes of Life and How to Get Out of Them*, writes about the world of education, the world of work, the world of retirement. He writes that life is really an orgy of learning, an orgy of work, an orgy of leisure. He feels we need to combine these phases of life as we live. In each phrase of life we need learning, work, and leisure. Once again, a balance for happiness and your spirit.

The Chinese character for crisis translates as dangerous opportunity. Every day we can dare to bring our spirit with us wherever we go, and live in a way that pleases us. When in doubt, ask: What is best for my spirit? How can I make this a dangerous opportunity for my creativity?

These are huge issues—work, creativity, and all. Give yourself the gift of a sixty-minute writing time today. Try one or all the exercises listed here. You'll be glad you gave yourself the extra time.

Exercises

1. Write about how you have used creative thinking in your work. How could you be creative in your present situation? What would you continue? Add? Change? Use *streaming* and then *listmaking*.

2. Make a line that stands for your life and make a dot for every five-year interval. What moments on this "life line" stand out in

sharpest detail to your memory. Note times of joy, sorrow, change including jobs, moves, friendships. What helped you preserve a constancy in your life? How can you bring that to your work situation in a creative way?

3. Now, using the same "life line," put a dot next to those times when you made important decisions. What was it you chose to do? What would happen if you had chosen another way? This may show constant values, consistent threads, and help you see what direction you want to go in.

4. On index cards write a "telegram" to ten people you know and tell them what to do about their job, for example: Find a focus and stick to it, or Speak up for what you want. Try to give the most helpful advice you can. Now see how this could relate to your situation and write about it.

DAY 4: THE BODY

Pablo Neruda once wrote, "Ever since I had an accident in which I broke a finger and couldn't use the typewriter for a few months, I have followed the custom of my youth and gone back to writing by hand. I discovered when my finger was better and I could type again that my poetry when written by hand was more sensitive, its plastic forms could change more easily. . . . The typewriter separated me from a deeper intimacy with poetry, and my hand brought me closer to that intimacy again." One of the most direct means for contacting the spirit is through the body—with a pen and paper.

John Steinbeck, author of *Grapes of Wrath*, writes: "You start out by putting words down and there are three things—you, the pen, and the page. Then gradually the three things merge until they are one and you feel about the page as you do about your arm. Only you love it more than you love your arm."

"There are short cuts to happiness, and dancing is one of them."
—*Vicki Baum*

129

When we write by hand, we become intimate with our wise voice and our spirit by noticing the intersection of our bodies and writing.

I wrote the following poem when I was physically tired. To me it is a very physical poem with a better future ahead sensed through the body and honoring the body's need for rest.

There is a Longing in Me

I cannot be a green growing
thing just now
gone, the curling bark
of springtime.

I want the river to cleanse me,
the fish to leap to my mouth,
want to dry my hair on the rock
of your body.

After my slumber, I'll rise:
we women always find the elbow to rise
walk through fields of goats and shadows,
the sky so everywhere above us.

I sometimes think of the line "always find the elbow to rise" and know that I will if I take care of my body. I'm glad a wisdom allows me to have time off from being super or even ordinary. Sometimes I can stop and let rain pour over me.

"The body says what words cannot."—Martha Graham

Of course, a critical part of our body awareness has to do with eros, with sex. A very ladylike friend told me that the only time she could relax these days was when she was having sex. I told her I hoped she had a lot of it. It was my prescription for her when I heard of her dilemmas in work and spirituality. We would write very sexual poetry for fun and read it to each other. I remember I wrote: "I'll cut my hair, / tattoo your ear, / stain your neck with snake tails, / caress you with enough nakedness / to confront the hunger of my changing." I was having a wild time with poetry while she wrote less and was in bed more.

The sexual revolution in the 1970s gave women the right to be sexual. The feminist movement gave women the right to interpret their sexuality and what it meant to them. These two movements took sexuality out of a man's interpretation and gave women the power to decide who they would like to be in terms of their involvement and sexuality. Women validated Freud's great intellect and his early writings of the subconscious while leaving his sexual theories behind as male sexism of the day.

There is an old Czechoslovakian folktale called the "The Wooden Maiden." It tells of how Gaia danced forth from the void and molded mountains along her spine and valleys in the hollows of her flesh. A rhythm of hills and stretching plains followed her contours. From her womb, six women and six men came. This is the tale of a woman's body becoming all that there is. You might want to write a myth for yourself and how you made a landscape you love.

Tell your story. Write it down, every aspect, and share the experience and your feelings about it. Share sitting down; share standing up. Believe your wise person is with you. Insight and action will help. If you are recovering from sexual abuse, admit that you need help and find a kind therapist to work with. With your therapist, develop a plan of how to deal with sexual recovery and make sure writing is part of the plan.

Surprise yourself and surprise the world. Let yourself have a sensual day where your body gets to have its way. Have a massage. Bathe in lavender oils for relaxation. Light a scented candle for calming. Smell the flowers in your garden. Write a prayer for all the trees on your

"When I had my daughter, I learned what the sound of one hand clapping is— it's a woman holding her infant in one hand and a pen in the other."
—*Kate Braverman*

walk through a woods. Wear silk to bed and sleep between satin sheets. Let the music of flutes lull you to sleep. God lives in every freckle, every wrinkle. Write about that.

Exercises

1. Using *streaming*, write down how your sexual partner(s) might want you to be different. What would this have to do with accepting your humanity?

2. Last night I saw the movie *The Buena Vista Social Club*, the documentary of Cuban musicians, many in their nineties. As they played the music they have loved since childhood, I could see a face of spirit coming through their bodies as music. Have you had experiences where in an art form you felt your body become more alive? Were you dancing, singing, making art? How does that affect your body sensations and sense of spirituality? Write about that.

3. Pick a photo of yourself that you particularly like or dislike. What do you remember about the state of your physical body? What does the picture show?

DAY 5: SPIRITUALITY

"We are a creature that is becoming conscious of itself. We can become the eyes and ears of nature, the feeling heart of God. Yet in the very miracle of having this consciousness, we become separated from the infinite self and help of interconnected wholeness that is the universe," writes Richard Moss in *The Second Miracle*. "What is being born in a new human being who is at once a separate self-awareness, individual and kindred with all. Self plus intuiting unnameable suchness as the "Beloved" of Rumi, the "I myself" of Whitman, the mysterious "other."

In Shelton B. Kopp's book *If You Meet the Buddha on the Road, Kill Him!*, the Zen master warns: "If you meet the Buddha on the road, kill him!" This admonition points up that no meaning that comes from outside of ourselves is real. The buddhahood of each of us has already been obtained. We need only recognize it. The only meaning in our lives is what we bring to them. Killing the Buddha on the road means destroying the hope that anything outside ourselves can be our master. "No one is any bigger than anyone else," Kopp says. "There are no mothers and fathers for grown-ups, only sisters and brothers. We must each give up the master, without giving up the search."

The idea that there is no master is what appeals to those of us who choose an eclectic spirituality. We sort through ideas and see what works for us. We may use a teacher or read books, but we check within ourselves to see if it is true for us. Our writing practice is a part of that process.

When I read of Buddha's life, I respond to his ideas of kindness and soft-heartedness. I like it that he lived until old age and knows about maturing and growing older. I like some of the Eastern influences; others, such as the sexism, I don't like. I respectfully take what I like and leave the rest. The gods live in many countries and many hands.

Hindus believe that their religion is without a beginning or end and there is a continuous process even preceding the existence of earth and many other worlds beyond. They insist that each person be guided by his or her individual spiritual experience and have no dictatorship in religious guidance.

These are teachings many of us can embrace. There is good in every religion. In spirituality we leave religion behind and instead take ideas with us on our journey. We combine what we know, feel, and sense and find a way that allows us to find contentment. As we find contentment, we help others around us find their ease.

My ex-Catholic friends sometimes pray to Mary or the black Madonna. They like the loving kindness of a woman. They need to see their woman-self as the image they believe in. A friend said, "I want a god that looks like me, a little old, a little plump, an inviting look on her face." I've had clients whose gods sit in a circle and invite them in, clients who dislike any talk of spirituality because it reminds them of past religious hurts but who use redwood trees for guidance. I've had the vision of more than one wise grandma or kind grandfather come to a client when they are in prayer, and offer their wide, safe lap.

Through writing, we come to know ourselves and our spiritual yearnings and truths. We learn what works for us. We allow our beliefs to change. We try to have an open mind and to listen to what other spiritual seekers say. We do what works for us just now. And keep on writing about it.

After writing regularly for a while, you'll find that if you skip a few days you miss it and the introspection that is a part of it. Something will be missing; we won't feel connected enough. And so we return to our journal and explore.

Luisah Teish, author of *Carnival of the Spirit,* talks about how she bought a kitchen timer because she needed structure to write. After her busy day of working and family, she wrote for exactly fifty minutes a day. I have a friend who writes in her journal in bed in the morning before she gets up. She sleeps with her shoes and the lights on so she is grounded all night. Kurt Vonnegut suggests that when you're writing a story you start somewhere closer to the middle, where there's action. He feels it's easier to write the main action or points and then go back and write the beginning. Although Vonnegut writes fiction, we can use his ideas and start at the heart of what we want to say—"Ouch" or "Hurray!"—and then off we go into streaming.

Exercises

1. What do you bring or not bring to your spiritual beliefs from the religious beliefs of your childhood? How does that help you now? What was it you had to overcome?

2. John Keats called the capacity to feel, listen, and wait when much is unknown as "negative capacity," a state when someone is capable of being in uncertainties, mysteries, doubts, without reaching after fact or reason. How have you employed "negative capacity" in your life? Explore how this could be a strength.

3. Observe your pet for ten minutes (or a bird outside your window) and write about spirituality. How are you like this animal or bird? What does it have to teach you?

DAY 6: SOLITUDE

One of my favorite things to do when I am alone and feeling a bit adrift is to slip into the place of contentment with solitude. Staying off the phone and continuing to read, garden, rest, or write helps the lonely feeling transform to one of connection to myself. It is a feeling that all is right with the world. I can focus on what is before me and feel fine. I am in harmony with myself. It is a delicious time of being with myself. I integrate solitude into each day if only for the last hour or so.

When I am writing in my journal, I often feel this shift from loneliness to solitude. You can't force it, but by focusing and continuing on you can open to that quiet place. Miraculously, after awhile, it's a feeling you will start to seek out. You'll be the person who says "I need time to myself so I can settle into myself. I need to journal," and the wise person you are will congratulate you.

"Pray that your loneliness may spur you into finding something to live for, great enough to die for."

—Dag Hammarskjold

Those times when no one knows where we are, those times when we are lost and not lost, help us know who we are and what belongs to us. Perhaps you had that feeling as you gazed at the Seine or stepped into a busy city street after a rain. "I am here. Alone. No one on earth knows where I am. I'm fine." This is the brilliant quality of solitude.

There is a spiritual force in small things, and solitude sometimes helps us see with clearer vision. Many of us can remember a time when the world was wonderfully quiet. It may have been a time when you were restless but you hung in and continued walking or writing. Suddenly you came to a place where there was a glow through the trees or a light in your mind. It is the shift from the ego self to the self of all things.

For a holiday present, I was given a calendar called *The Writer's Life*. Each month there is a photograph and a quotation from a famous writer. One quotation by the poet Rita Dove points to the importance of quiet and nature. She writes: "What I love about my cabin—what I always forget that I love until I open the door and step into it—is the absolute quiet. Oh, not the dead silence of a studio. A silence so physical that you begin to gasp for air. This is a silence of the world: birds shifting weight on branches, the branches squeaking against other twigs, the deer hooosching through the woods. . . . It's a silence where you can hear your blood in your chest, if you choose to listen."

As much as we love connection to others, we can't chat and write. We have to choose. One way to do this is to say I love this but I love that more just now. It might mean I'd love to go to the beach with you but I'd love to have a chapter done at the end of the weekend more. Again, we hold both and choose one.

Another beloved quote from the calendar is from Dorothy West. She writes: "I'm a writer. I don't cook and I don't clean. . . . Dear child, this place is a mess—my papers are everywhere. It would be exhausting to clean up! When I was seven, I said to my mother, may I close the door? And she said, yes, but why do you want to close the door? And I said because I want to think. And when I was eleven, I said to my mother, may I lock my door? And she said yes, but why do you want to lock your door. And I said because I want to write."

Dorothy West reminds us to think about what's most important and to mostly do that. She reminds us to use humor and do what we love. Solitude gives her solace that puts her in a good place to create.

Jane Bowles, in her book *In the Summer House*, writes: ". . . sometimes when I wake up at night with a strange feeling of isolation . . . as if I'd fallen off the cliffs and landed miles away from everything that was close to my heart, even my griefs and my sorrows don't seem to belong to me. Nothing does—as if a shadow had passed over my whole life and made it dark. . . . But if we occupy ourselves while the shadow passes, it passes swiftly enough and scarcely leaves a trace of our daily lives. . . ." She asks us to have courage and let the spirit move the difficult and lonely times through us.

"Spirituality," writes Christina Baldwin, "is the sacred center out of which all life comes, including Mondays and Tuesdays and rainy Saturday afternoons in all their mundane and glorious detail. . . . The spiritual journey is the soul's life co-mingling with the ordinary life." Baldwin continues: "Spiritual love is a position of standing with one hand extended in the universe and one hand extended into the world, letting ourselves be a conduit for passing energy" (*Life's Companion*, 1990). We can feel this best when we are least expecting it, walking on a boardwalk alone at night, waking from sleep feeling the touches of angels from a dream. Create solitude in your life and you'll prepare the stage for the magnificent to happen.

The gods live in us and everywhere. In solitude we can look out the window and let the vulture in us be caged. We can know that we have enough. We can rest assured that we are more than we ever dreamed, that we are accepted. Through solitude we can know we are welcomed.

The soul, like the moon,

is new, and always new again.

—Sarah Orne Jewett

137

Exercises

1. Write about what scares you about being alone. Remember to include childhood fears and present-day concerns.

2. Imagine being in your special place with your wise person, *gazing into the waters.* Let her explain to you how solitude will enhance your life and what you could say to help yourself.

3. Make up a myth that tells how you are comforted at night. Try *clustering* on the word *comfort* and use some of the words in your myth. You might say a cloud comes from heaven to hold you and—. Or perhaps a spirit of angels band together and—.

DAY 7: REWARDING YOURSELF— GIFTS OFFERED

"No object is mysterious.

The mystery is your eye."

—*Elizabeth Bowen*

All week we've been talking about becoming whole by having love and friendship, work and creativity, a healthy attitude toward our physical body, and spirituality and solitude in our lives. Today, go to some lovely building nearby and notice the grounds, the building, and what it holds. Notice the people in the vicinity. Notice the weather around the building. Write in your journal how this makes a whole experience. Note what you are especially drawn to and what you learn today.

WEEK 8: THE GREAT SIGH

Peace of Mind

"Every time we take the time to smile, we relax our minds and body, and we help ourselves and those around us touch peace. But it is not always easy to smile. There is so much suffering in the world. . . . [We] can take the time to notice the wonders of life that are within us and all around us, we will plant seeds of peace in ourselves and in the world. If we are mindful in each moment, we will plant seeds of peace in ourselves wherever we go in the world, and these seeds will surely blossom," said Thich Nhat Hanh, a Vietnamese monk and great teacher, at a talk at his retreat in Plum Village, France.

My dear friend Robert, who lives as a layperson in Plum Village, spends his afternoons in walking meditation look-

"People from another planet without flowers would think we must be mad with joy the whole time to have such things about us."
—*Iris Murdoch*

ing at a flower arrangement in the greenhouse and then writes his experience in his journal. He feels more anxiety than he knew was possible; he feels more peace than he knew was possible. All things. He is. We are.

We overcome anger through loving kindness. We overcome hurt by doing good. We overcome lies with truth. We overcome anxiety by letting it be. Use writing regularly to help you create the inner

"What God expects us
to attempt, he also enables
us to achieve."
—Stephen Olford

harmony and peace that will allow you to become the person you really are. Trust that you will not be given more than you can handle, even if it doesn't seem so at the moment. Yes, the goddess is there for you at all times. Just turn to her and write what we know is already within us. Explore what that means to you. It's true.

I grew up near the Amish in Pennsylvania and admired their life

of simplicity. The mildness and patience of the people surprised me.

I remember that being around the Amish felt different from what

I felt being around the church people I knew. The Amish felt more

in the body while the church members in my home town felt more

in the head. It makes me want to dig in the dirt and make sure I am

connected with growing things.

DAY 1: FORGIVENESS

"If you haven't
forgiven yourself
something,
how can you
forgive others?"
—Dolores Huerta

An old African proverb says "The ax forgets, the tree remembers." This is true after we are hurt and need to process the experience. In time, however, forgiving without forgetting is not the energy we want to carry in the body. To have peace of mind we must forget that place that continues to cut us off from our spirit. Anything that increases separation within us shatters our soul or in some form diminishes its strength. Holism cannot tolerate nonforgiveness.

In *Forgiving the Unforgivable*, Beverly Flanigan tells us that we must first claim the injury, the separation from self. "The task of claiming is to say, 'This is my injury—no one else's. Other people may have been hurt, too. But I can't do anything about that. I must forgive this injury because this is the one that harmed me.' " The separating out brings into focus even more clearly the course ahead for the remainder of the forgiving process. It takes time, attention to tasks, and relief from demands on resources. We must separate the memories of the past injuries it may trigger. For example, being taken off a project at work is not the same as being left out by your siblings as a child. Sound silly? Maybe, but our subconscious links events together by similar feelings.

There is such a thing as the healthy use of blame, of course. It separates you from the injurer and brings into focus your intentions and those of the injurer. The process of healthy blaming—filtering, weighing, fact-finding—helps us to see how all involved parties contributed. Through this process we can: (1) Make the choice to release the injurer from debt. (2) Make the choice to cut the bonds that still hold us to the injurer—this will set both you and the injurer free. (3) Make a choice to look ahead, not back.

In *The Seat of the Soul*, Gary Zukav writes: "Forgiveness is not a moral issue. It is an energy dynamic. Forgiveness means you do not carry the baggage of the experience. The experience that you do not forgive is still with you, it is like agreeing to wear dark, gruesome sunglasses that distort everything, and it is who you are forced every day to look at through those contaminated lenses because you have chosen to keep them."

Walt Kelly, in a quote from his cartoon *Pogo*, says, "We have met the enemy, and he is us." We must begin by forgiving ourselves. Forgiveness means you do not hold others responsible for your experiences. A client, Kent, allowed a girlfriend to manipulate him for several years after she asked him to move out. She wanted to be sexual but she didn't want day-to-day intimacy. When she chose to live with someone else, he was furious. In time, Kent saw that he allowed her to be indirect with him because of his hope. His work was to forgive and release the critical judgment of himself.

Other times we truly have no part in the wrongs done to us. In situations of oppression, for instance. Someone's hate of the otherness in himself causes him to single us out because of the color of our skin or some other difference. Even if we are of the majority culture, few of us live through childhood without some disrespect and hurt. Anger is a natural response to being wronged in this way. To forgive before we find our anger is not an empowering process. We must recognize oppression and abuse and say it is wrong. It is not our fault. It is unjust. But by recognizing that we are not at fault, and by calling out the truth as we see it, we are sometimes able to let go.

At day care, my friend's granddaughter, Steffie, was bitten by another child. She told her grandma when they got home. As she described what happened, this mild, happy child tore two pages out of her favorite book and broke three crayons. Later the grandma noticed she had drawn big blue and red swirls on the wall. Angry, yes. Rightfully? Sure. And my friend noted that Steffie took it out on her own prized possessions, and that it was appropriate to find the "bad" outside of Steffie. So, grandma took Steffie to day care the next day so Steffie could face her tormenter. The other little one said he was sorry but my friend didn't think he really remembered. But since Steffie had expressed her anger, she was now beyond it—and interested in getting on the merry-go-round. She had released it, and it no longer controlled her.

When we have been the one doing wrong, it can help to write out what we are going to say in apology. This will give us greater clarity on just what we're sorry for. We can then apologize with sincerity and move forward.

Those to whom amends are made can ask for the spirit's help to praise the other for the difficult task of owning up to his or her part in the interaction. We can respect the attempts of others to do this. We can say, honestly, "I can't forgive you yet, but I will work on forgiveness. Thank you for coming to me and saying what you did."

A client who was married to a police officer said his gun was suddenly around in the bedroom as they broke up. He was intimidating her and she knew it. She asked his partner to talk to him and the gun disappeared. It was a very difficult breakup, but it was the best for both of them. Three years later they were at the same fund-raising event and she looked across the room at him and there he was looking at the ice cubes in his empty glass. For some reason she found that little act very silly and endearing. She remembered how sometimes he felt overwhelmed in a crowd and would want to go home.

She remembered times he wore his teddy bear slippers as he relaxed watching television. She checked inside and realized she could forgive him. She knew she could because their relationship and the breakup didn't hurt or scare her anymore.

He had told her he was sorry he had frightened her and was not there in their relationship to help with the children. She had written "I wish you well far, far away from me" over and over, and now he could be in the same room and she wished him well. She felt by forgiving him she had regained a piece of her authentic power, the part of her that she had allowed him to dominate. And certainly the children would benefit from more harmony.

She now believed in the spirit in small things and was mindful in all her relationships to share equally and not allow someone to have more than their share. She was around people who made her feel good about herself and life had taught her that she had a spirit to help her forgive well and live well.

Sonja Johnson, in her book *From Housewife to Heretic*, writes: "I have resigned myself to the fact that Rick is always going to hate me because he has committed a grave offense against me, for which he will never forgive me." Check within yourself and see if you can find a place where you have injured someone and now cannot be around them because you cannot forgive yourself. I immediately think of someone who I judged too fast and harshly and said what I thought. When I think of her, I shrink a little.

"Forgiveness is the act of admitting we are like other people." —*Christina Baldwin*

Sometimes journaling how we are like those we don't forgive helps us to see our humanness. We can explore how even the best of us are flawed. In the worst of us, there is some redeeming feature. We write to look at ourselves objectively and then give the same respect to others. We ask what might others be trying to protect?

"Forgiveness is the answer to the child's dream of a miracle by which what is broken is made whole again, what is soiled is again made clean."
—*Dag Hammarskjold*

Peace of mind is a choice, not a consequence. We might try choosing mildness instead of criticism, no matter what anybody did. Never mind them, what is better for us? Isn't that selfish? Yes, and it is also wise and good. We can look around at our own inner garden. What a tangle I find sometimes and ask my wise woman to help me.

"I have to be willing to forgive, but I cannot will myself to forgive. I can forgive with my mind, but forgiveness is finally a matter of the heart. And forgiveness of the heart comes from the wise person not from me. My part is to be willing to accept it."

—Madeleine L'Engle

In the novel *Bone,* Fae Myenne Ng writes that in Chinese, *get long* is translated as "to get along, to make do"; it was about having a long view, which was endurance, and a long heart, which was hope. That's what I want us to do, to learn how to make do with these memories and with a long heart, forgive.

Exercises

1. Spiritual acceptance means asking hard questions about our own behavior. How often have you acted with less compassion when you were out of sorts? List those to whom you owe amends. Write what you would say. Take a chance to change your energy and possibly the relationships and write or tell that person.

2. How do you see yourself? Write down nouns as fast as you can that describe you. Dialogue with your wise person or a teacher and see how the wise one sees you. What's the difference? Write down some affirmations to affirm your own true self.

3. For one week, write down the first thoughts you have in the morning, especially noting if you have anything unresolved with another or are holding any grudge. Each morning, write a prayer to help your spirit live with the concern and not just your ego. Or just let the spirit write a response to your morning thoughts.

4. Write a thank-you note to yourself for all your contributions.

DAY 2: ALL WE CAN HANDLE

One of the hardest things for me is to be confronted with a difficult situation and not know what to do. I sleep on not knowing. I tell a friend without having or wanting any answer. I see the crones around the table and hear them say they have learned that they can handle what life brings. Life has been harder than I ever imagined, with still-births and miscarriages, alienation and despair. Life has been better than I ever imagined, with beaches and city lights and raven nights. I am still here as are you.

Today, treat the day as if you can handle anything. This attitude will bring you peace of mind. Don't just make promises but bring in that feeling of "I can." When you feel as if you can't cope, slow down and see what you can do differently. Write about it. Remember, doing the same things will produce the same result. When our hand is on the page, the spirit is with us always, sometimes hidden, sometimes apparent, but she is there. Let the spirit know we know she gave us strength enough to handle what we are given and ask for deeper knowing and guidance.

Victor Hugo once wrote: "Sorrow is a fruit. God does not allow it to grow on a branch that is too weak to bear it." It is amazing to watch survivors of a fire accept a blanket and wrap a loved one in it. It's heartwarming to watch someone save and plan and change their life to allow for family time or creativity.

I included this section in *Peace of Mind* because I feel it is the bottom line of peaceful and happy living. We can't control what life will bring. Life doesn't measure out things in fair increments and say, "This year your brother was ill. I'll wait 'til next year to have you hate your job." Life is energy and it happens and just rolls on its way. It's our job not to be rolled over by it. A spiritual perspective will help in many ways. You have the spirit to write. You have a spirit to hold you. You are not alone. The spirit will ask you to connect with others. The wise person wants you to write and learn from your experience.

"The words loved me and I loved them in return."
—Sonia Sanchez

"When it comes to the pinch, human beings are heroic."
—George Orwell

"We have to dare to be ourselves, however frightening or strange that self may prove to be."
—May Sarton

"It is a good thing to have all the props pulled out from under us occasionally. It gives us some sense of what is rock under our feet, and what is sand," writes Madeleine L'Engle, author of *Glimpses of Grace*. To face a difficult situation and to survive and even thrive deepens our sense of self. The spirit hovers with its joyous wings saying, "See there, I will help you."

Exercises

1. *Dialogue* with a secret fear of trouble in yourself.

2. Make a list of daily, weekly, yearly rituals that help you organize your life and give you a feeling of continuity and predictability. For example, what are your morning rituals? What do you do at the end of the day? What holiday rituals do you have? What do your rituals say about you? What does your spirit say about the use of rituals?

3. Make a list of what difficulties you have handled well in your life. Make a list of those you wish you had done better. (I remember a friend saying she couldn't hang in well with someone dying until the third time.) How does your life experience help you?

DAY 3: HUMOR

By allowing us to change tragedy to comedy, humor helps our peace of mind. It shows our resilience. It helps us discharge the energy of the feeling. "It couldn't have gotten any worse," we might say with a laugh. Or, at the end of a disgusting day, we see a man in the wind step into a cardboard box blowing across the wide sidewalk. It could have been us. And we know it could be the last straw of a bad day that sets us to crying or laughing. Better laughing, we think. At least with laughter we'll be able to go on, get to our car, and perhaps tell the story some day.

"Your crown has been bought and paid for. All you must do is put it on your head."

—*James Baldwin*

Humor helps us to cope better. It's a human connection to tell a friend the worst of things, especially when you both know it will be okay and you'll be fine. There have been times in my life when, as the bird shit hit my foot, I've instantly thought, another "Sherrill" story. My friend Sherrill will appreciate how I didn't need this today.

When someone trips or falls in a hole we may try not to laugh, but sometimes it's a relief to discharge these shadow feelings. Too bad for that guy! A friend, after settling her mom in the only nursing home that would take her because she is violent and bites, called and asked me to come over and shoot her. I understood.

It's a good discipline to write not only when we're distressed but when we have something humorous to say. It records our wit and the irony of life. It shows our ability to cope. It can be a real help to reread passages of humor and remember that we can feel this way, too. Our spirit sings best with laughter and tears.

A client phoned and said her car lurched as she left work to come for her session and she had to take it to the garage. The mechanic said a spark plug had come out. She thought it was a metaphor for the way she was feeling, and from then on, when she was feeling "done in," she'd tell me her spark plug came out. Keeping these metaphors in our journal can help us keep a record of feeling life.

Laughter is a great way to connect to others. A nurse practitioner told me that the doctor she works for, feeling particularly overloaded one day, stuck his head into the employees' room and said, "Quick. Quick. Get a doctor." I know I've sometimes felt like yelling "Call the shrink."

After a messy breakup, it can help to laugh about (and write down) all the bad habits of the ex-partner or spouse. Try not to threaten to

"We are not amused!"

—*Queen Victoria*

"He who laughs, lasts!"

—*Mary Pettibone Poole*

"Laugh and the world laughs with you, snore and you sleep alone."

—*Mrs. Patrick Campbell*

read them in public. It can be comic relief to hear that a former spouse who never wears panties is now dating a minister.

In *Stressed Is Desserts Spelled Backwards*, Brian Luke Seaward writes that humor comes to us from the same root as the words *fluid* or *moisture*. Humor is about having a fluid spirit. When we sit at the computer and growl after spending a day organizing our computer files, we know we still have our humor. When a friend calls and says this is a sympathy call and lists all the terrible things that are happening at work today reminding you of a script of "Ally McBeal," you know she's using humor to cope. When we make light of a bad situation, it takes the edge off. We separate ourselves from the problem.

Regardless of its source, humor makes us feel better. The average child laughs three hundred to four hundred times a day; an adult, fifteen times; a hospital patient, one time. Informal studies show that people heal faster when they laugh. We've all heard of people watching comedies as they recuperate and they do feel better.

I have a client who keeps a joke journal. His goal is to be able to tell jokes with his friends. What is funny is the way he can't keep them straight. And the way he laughs so hard before I know what's funny. Whatever he's doing, it's the right thing for his spirit. I'm sure his wise person would say, "Keep on. The impulse to laugh is from God. Keep on."

Exercises

1. Write about some situations that feel especially difficult right now. Explore the ways humor might help you cope better. Even if that seems impossible, by writing awhile you'll put the possibility into your life.

2. Go through magazines and find pictures that make you laugh. Write what you think resonates in you about that picture? Is it a memory? Which one? Is it shadow stuff? What? How can humor help you know yourself better?

3. Write about some experiences humor has put to rest.

DAY 4: GRATITUDE

Yesterday we wrote about humor, but humor isn't the only emotion that has a positive effect on us. Emotions such as gratitude and love and joy also have a positive effect on our physical health and peace of mind. Whereas stress dumps high levels of adrenaline into the bloodstream, raises blood pressure, potentially damaging arteries and the heart itself, when we bathe our spirits with openheartedness, we bathe our bodies with good hormones.

Gratitude can enhance the immune system, which enables the body to resist diseases and recover more quickly from illness through the release of endorphins in the bloodstream. Endorphins are the body's natural painkillers. Among other effects, they stimulate dilation of the blood vessels, which lead to a relaxed heart. When we are physically well, peace of mind is easy to maintain and gratitude is the attitude that assures this.

Start a gratitude journal in a beautiful blank book; write with a lovely ink pen. Save the everyday notebooks for streaming and make this one luscious. Try to remember to write in it each day. Write two things you are grateful for and try to have as many new things as possible: an event, a creative thought, a feeling, a tree at your window. When you need moral reinforcement, reread your gratitude journal.

Gratitude is an antidote to bitterness and resentment. One client, Jeanine, felt bitterness grow because her life felt too hard and disappointments too numerous. She felt she deserved better than the treatment she received from her friends and co-workers. She felt unlucky and victimized. She didn't have the

"There are only two ways to live your life. One is as though nothing is a miracle. The other is as if everything is."
—Albert Einstein

"What you praise you increase."
—Catherine Ponder

149

insight that her flash temper response was an element in her problems with people.

Indeed, her life was in a difficult place and she was suffering. She needed support to cry and get angry but her attention needed to be on her suffering not on bitterness. Giving attention to suffering also meant to sit and acknowledge it. To have it witnessed. By writing about it, she healed. By making lists of what she was grateful for, she healed. Ask yourself: What are you grateful for in the physical world? The spiritual world? Write about that in your gratitude journal.

In *Everyday Sacred: A Woman's Journey Home,* Sue Bender writes about making ceramic bowls. She says it's not the bowls we're making, it's ourselves. "Most of us are like those Zen tea bowls, uneven, cracked, imperfect. And our harsh judge keeps wishing we were perfect. The difference is the tea bowls are revered just as they are."

In Latin, imperfect means unfinished, not unflawed. We can be grateful for what we are. We can be pleased with ourselves and still know we aren't finished. We may be making writing instead of bowls but the idea holds: We are still forming.

Bender writes: "In many religious traditions a monk sets out with his begging bowl and an exchange is made. Food is placed in his bowl and he accepts the offering gratefully. The offering gives him strength to do his work and, in return, he gives guidance and wisdom. Who gives? Who receives?" What is there to be grateful about here? We fill and digest. We can walk away with overflowing bellies and gratitude.

If you want something to be grateful about, create an atmosphere where good can happen. Be generous to someone you don't know. Reach out to a friend. Volunteer to feed the homeless. Learn new songs or poems to share.

If you find that you are not feeling gratitude for much in your life, start small. "Before you taste anything, recite a blessing," writes Rabbi

Akiva. This way of thinking can become a habit. So can ungrateful thinking. Try the following exercises and see how you can change the way you think and how it affects your mood and your days.

Exercises

1. Take time at the end of the day to change your nongrateful thoughts to grateful thoughts. If you're stuck thinking about someone else's good fortune, try writing such things as "I can be quite lucky myself," or "Good things happen to me. Just last week . . ." Then read over your list of grateful thoughts and do *gazing into the waters* to relax and let the more positive thoughts sink into your subconscious. Do some *streaming* to deepen these grateful thoughts. How are they really true? What do you need to let go of in order to more fully know this?

2. Write a list of nouns as fast as you can for three minutes. The list might look like this: tea, chalk, computer, flower, hospital, bird, mother, sister, aunt, bed, tree, sky, finger, glasses, bowl, rubber band, clip, pen, sun, shadow, clock. See what insights the nouns offer and be grateful for those. I can see mine are about the writing life and concern about my mom in the hospital. I might write about how writing enriches my life and gives me focus in times of worry. I might write how grateful I am to have a loving relationship with my mom, or gratitude for the healing we have done over the years between us. I might write about how grateful I was that her visit last month was a happy one. I might write about the miracle that we both lived long enough to grow and change.

   "Keep breathing."

   —Sophie Tucker

3. Ask yourself: What would I do if I forgave? and write down the answers.

DAY 5: SIMPLICITY

"In the end, what affects your life most deeply are things too simple to talk about."

—*Nell Blaine*

Imagine what you would do if your personal life were simpler. You'd spend time with those people who understood your spiritual path and with whom you could share. You'd limit other people to an infrequent "have to" list because they are family or because they are ill and you offered to help. You'd gently let go of relationships that don't work for you and spend time with those with whom you can be yourself. You'd trust your intuition. And, don't forget, you'd clean up old relationships so unsolved feelings wouldn't drain your energy.

Where can you begin to simplify?

You can have the courage to say I have enough and actually don't need all I have. It is simpler to live small. It's easier not to have to hire help. I don't miss my four-bedroom, three-bath home, and I certainly won't miss cleaning it. I'm happier doing what I want in a simple way than having money and living a life I don't like.

How might you simplify? By drinking water, packing your lunch, and not driving over the speed limit, you simplify. By buying a smaller house with a smaller yard or a stone and shrub yard that needs no care. By planting vegetables one year and cut flowers the next. By selling the plane, wearing mostly black and white and shades of red, keeping your wardrobe simple. By eating meals of cottage cheese and bread and fruit and raw vegetables, making a big pot of vegetable soup and eating from the pot with a different salad all week. By using the car phone for real emergencies only, combining trips into the city with errands and friends and culture; otherwise, stay in your own community. By enjoying the library and nights of reading, turning off the answering machine after eight each night. To simplify your finances, make it a priority to pay off your debt and don't incur more. Rethink your buying by noting for two months what you buy. You'll be better able to see your buying habits. Decide on how many pairs of winter shoes you need and stop. Change the way you shop and use as many one-stop shopping stores or malls as you can.

"I have a simple philosophy. Fill what's empty. Empty what's full. Scratch where it itches."

—*Alice Roosevelt Longworth*

Throw away anything you haven't used for a year. Or box things and date them, as a neighbor of mine does. He says he checks the box after a year and throws out what he didn't use that year. This way he's had a year to think about it. Do whatever works for you. A creative and soulful mind would prefer lack of clutter. There's a desk sign that reads "A creative mind needs a tidy desk." Simplicity allows new things to happen and gives room for the soul to turn around and invent.

Use your computer more or less, depending on what would be simpler for your job. Notice how much time you waste on phone calls or busy work by blocking out your time more clearly. Choose work that you want to do so you can enjoy it more.

When I think of Nelson Mandela, the former president of South Africa, I think of how simply he lives his life. He is a man who has *Obuntubotho*, the essence of being human. In Yiddish the word to describe him would be mensch, someone who others want to be around because of his kindness. Fight the desire to be seen as fascinating.

"There is no cure for birth or death save to enjoy the interval."
—*George Santayana*

Live your life as yourself; you need no toys or engines or fancy boots. "I believe we would be happier to have a personal revolution in our individual lives and go back to simpler living and more direct thinking. It is the simple things of life that make living worthwhile, the sweet fundamental things such as love and duty, work and rest and living close to nature," writes Etty Hillesum in her dairies.

Here is a vision of simplicity by Sulak Sivaraksa in *Seeds of Peace*: " . . . a truly developed city would not be distinguished by a multitude of skyscrapers, but by the values attendant in its growth: simplicity, comfort, and respect for the community of life around it. People would enjoy a simpler, healthier and less costly diet, lower on the food chain and without toxic additives or wasteful packaging. Animals would no long be annihilated at the rate of 500,000 per hour to be an option on every menu. A new work ethic could be to enjoy our work and work in harmony with others, as opposed to getting ahead of others and having a miserable time doing it."

He continues, "What is most basic is to work on ourselves. Movement starts with individual and moves to village. We need an inner

realization concerning greed, hatred, and delusion, and an outer realization concerning the impact these tendencies have on society and
the planet."

E. F. Schumacher reminds us in *Small Is Beautiful* that "Western economics encourages the maximization of material gain without regard
for people. He presents Buddhist economics as a study of economics
as if people mattered, saying that Buddhist concepts of development
avoid gigantism, especially of machines, which tend to control rather
than serve human beings. If we can avoid the extreme of bigness and
greed, we may be on a middle path of Buddhist development, creating a world in which industry and agriculture are meaningful and satisfying for all beings."

*"Simplicity is making
the journey with just
baggage enough."
—Anonymous*

Simplicity means different things to different people. Start in the
way that makes sense for you. Try on even more. Write and imagine
a life with less appliances and electronics. Ask the wise person you are
to help you. Imagine a life where the value system was built around
care for the individual and the community. A system where writing
becomes true home, a place of solitude and comfort.

Exercises

1. Write down the following sentence: "I am right where I am supposed to be." If you believed this, how would it simplify your life?
   Write lists of how you could simplify your life in categories of
   Home, Lifestyle, including shopping and wardrobe, Personal Relationships, and Healthy Eating.

2. Write about the following: What would be the threat in simplifi-
   cation? The happiness? What would the process be to simplify and
   find your way to happiness?

3. Take a short story you like and write it out as a poem with few
   words.

DAY 6: HAPPINESS

"Happiness comes of the capacity to feel deeply, to enjoy simply, to think freely, to risk life, to be needed," says English novelist, Margaret Storm Jameson. Perhaps paddling down a river makes you feel deeply connected. To write in your journal alone in the woods at the side of the river can be transcendent. Some find camping a way to once again enjoy the closeness to nature they enjoyed as a freely thinking child. To wind surf, to write fiction and publish it, to volunteer to feed the hungry may be ways for you to risk and feel needed. Walking in the snow past store windows in the city may help you feel the pulse of the city and be happy. Whatever it is, the activity will trigger the energy within that is waiting to be expressed.

"The grand essentials to happiness in this life are something to do, something to love and something to hope for."

—Joseph Addison

Many of us have lived through hardship not realizing that happiness was the goal. We spend years trying to get by, to cope, to bear it. We might pray just to handle things well.

Ask your spirit to help you see that you can have troubles but not be a troubled person. Write what makes you happy and do those activities. Doing what you love helps your body remember the good feeling it had in happiness.

"Happiness is the meaning and the purpose of life, the whole aim and end of human existence."

—Aristotle

Use affirmations and write over and over statements that feel useful to you. "I am a happy person. I love the earth and sky. I love colors. I love people. I am blessed with a good mind and good health. Happiness is mine." Or "I am happy. I am a part of all things." Or "I will be happy today if I follow the voice of my heart. I accept wisdom as a gift from my higher power. I am blessed."

Just for fun and for truth let's think of happiness as our duty. There is so much suffering in the world, we are under obligation to put out the energy of our happiness. Our energy blends in with the energy of the world, as Alan Watts said, and we can change the mix. I go to a café near my office and sometimes I am so happy, I feel as if I could adopt the young woman with green hair. She notices my energy and comes right over to talk to me. I know she feels my happiness and connection to her. Those moments are like an unexpected gift of spirit.

There is, of course, such a thing as false happiness. False happiness is seeking pleasures that are not in our own interest, such as too much partying or too much wandering around for sexual experiences. Make sure your pleasures bring you no hardship. The route to happiness is different for each of us. I loved hearing the words of Robert Louis Stevenson when I was a child, "The world is so full of a number of things, I'm sure we should be as happy as kings."

A client just returned from a two-week retreat at a camp in southern California where she rested and learned about correct eating. She had been large-sized since she was a child and was tired of the cycle of dieting and overeating. She ate healthfully for the two weeks and learned how to combine food and how food is digested. She came back with information she felt she had always needed.

She seemed radiant and happy. She had used her vacation to help herself and she felt empowered by all the new information she had received. She said the surprise was that she was one of the few overweight people there. Most were there because of cancer. It put her struggle into its true perspective. The experience was life-changing even if she never lost a pound. She did, however, and I thought also became more connected to herself and others.

One of the things that was recommended at the camp was to write each evening what you were grateful for and to put those things into your dream time. She was surprised how the attention was not on body image but on the idea that happiness comes from taking care of yourself, and from who you are and your inner life. They were trying to teach that happiness is a grateful aptitude, the ability to enjoy life as it is. The eating tools were pretty simple: knowledge, peace of mind, happiness.

We can seek happiness on purpose. We can write for happiness.

We can set up a happiness altar and write before it. Happiness must

have permission to come and go. It cannot be captured.

Remember, indulging in positive thinking if we haven't dealt with our feelings can be dangerous. So always try to deal with your feelings by writing about them and then affirm your right to be happy.

We are responsible for our own happiness. Our health may be uncertain, our paycheck small, our friend ill in the hospital, and yet we can be happy. Situations and others may worry us, but they cannot make us feel any particular way. Yes, we can be triggered. Yes, it's easier to be around someone who is polite. But we always have a choice how to respond.

When you ride public transportation, for example, you see edges of much heartache and much disaster. You can say no to the heartache and still keep your heart open.

Each time you are happy you are doing the spirit's work on earth. The price for not connecting with your spirit is to be shaken in the wind each day when you have the choice to be joyful and sheltered. Use your heart as your guide.

"Happiness is not a station to arrive at, but a manner of traveling."
—*Margaret Lee Runbeck*

"Be happy. It's one way of being wise."
—*Colette*

"My heart is like a singing bird."—*Christina Rossetti*

With writing and the spirit's help, you can learn what makes you feel lucky. Add these to your life. They remind your body what happiness feels like, and with memory, it's easier to re-create this feeling.

Exercises

1. Write how you would literally put something together—a cake, a dress. Now take this process and do the same for spiritual process and the journey to happiness.

2. Choose a person who seems happy to you and describe him or her by using your senses. What do your senses know that you probably couldn't prove? How could you be more like this person?

3. Sort through a group of magazines at home or at a bookstore and write down the article titles on the covers, such as "The Guide to the Flame," "Prophets of Boom," or "Activists Making Peace." Choose an article name and write your own article describing how happiness was entered. How does this relate to your life and spiritual search?

4. Write down times of happiness. Write down things that make you happy. Decide when next to do some of these things.

DAY 7: REWARDING YOURSELF— THE CHOICE

For your reward this week, take a walk and notice fences. Notice the variety of materials and sizes. If you think of fences as holding something in or keeping something out, how would this relate to peace of mind? Now choose fences that represent you at different times and write about that. Use *clustering* if you wish to get started.

"Living on borders and in margins, keeping intact one's shifting and multiple identity

and integrity, is like trying to swim in a new element, an 'alien' element."

—Gloria Anzaldua

WEEK 9: FLOWING INTO OTHER CHANNELS

Appreciating the Cycles of Life

Anaïs Nin writes: "We do not grow absolutely, chronologically. We grow sometimes in one dimension, and not in another, unevenly. We grow partially. We are relative. We are mature in one realm, childish in another. The past, the present, and future mingle and pull us backward, forward, or fix us in the present. We are made up of layers, cells, constellations." Once we know this, peace of mind circles us always because we are always growing.

I have a client who is wise and soulful after the loss of her mother at sixteen. She also wears red plastic skirts and loves rap music and, after grieving, can be her young self again. A new friend in her sixties who is a well-known sculptor is learning how to express herself in words. She sees in images and is looking for a way to translate that. The cycles of life can give us time to be much more than we dreamed. The spirit can help you find peace in each stage.

> *"Whether it's the best of times or the worst of times, it's the only time we've got."*
> —Art Buchwald

"But some people change themselves so much that there is something new to be observed in them forever."

—Jane Austen

Transitions are the winding road of life. There's a time that comes after every beginning and plateau and ending. There's a time before a beginning again. To acknowledge that change will come is to better help us enjoy beginnings and plateaus with gratitude. When change comes, we bow to the maker and allow it to lead us.

Let today be your miracle. Notice what is in front of you and give thanks for it. An old Eskimo proverb says "Yesterday is ashes; tomorrow wood. Only today does the fire burn brightly." Make up some proverbs of your own if you want.

"About the only thing that comes to us without effort is old age," says American writer Gloria Pitzer (*Reader's Digest* 1979). Growing old is a process of accommodation, adjustment, and renewal. Aging of any kind can be digested as a human occurrence that is accepted and welcomed. I believe it isn't until we lose youth that we understand how wonderful the other cycles of life can be. We can write about flowing with the river, we can be the seasons, the changing tides. We wish for ourselves to be delivered to another shore where there are berries and scrubs we've never seen before. We can pray that we are not stuck in any age or place but that we move on to the summons of our spirit.

"I have learned to make my mind large, as the universe is large, so that there is room for paradoxes."

—Maxine Hong Kingston

Edna St. Vincent Millay writes: "Into the darkness they go, the wise and the lovely." A client recently told me she hoped the poet was wise and lovely at her death. Recently I read a quote by the poet Linda Hogan: "Death is running me ragged." Life can be hard and the fear of death can make it feel even harder. Maybe we can put down our quivering heart long enough to make use of death's coming in our life. We can read and write and come to terms with the unknown the best we can. We can practice endings.

What I love about rebirth is that it is a chapter that can be written over and over. Any tale of yours will do. Any story tells a possibility of what it might be like. Write a poem of afterlife and make it true. Believe what you believe. But believe in something for your own solace and change it when you want. Let your belief in rebirth fit your feelings today. What is important is that you explore your spirit. What is important is that you write. "All is fish that comes to the literary net," writes Louisa May Alcott in her journal. "Goethe puts his joys and sorrows into poems, I turn my adventures into bread and butter." Whatever fish come to your net, let writing help you explain to yourself the things you do not understand.

DAY 1: PAST

How can we face the present or the future with our past

weighing us down as rocks wrapped in cloth lugged on our back?

When the past has the color of yearning, how can we be free

enough to see the yellow of the bird's wing or the pad of red

on the blackbird's wing?

"History," Stephen said,
"is a nightmare from which
I am trying to awake."
—James Joyce

Ellen Glasgow, in *The Woman Within: An Autobiography*, writes: "But there is, I have learned, no permanent escape from the past. It may be an unrecognized law of our nature that we should be drawn back, inevitably, to the place where we have suffered the most." The past waits for us to return to release old hurts so we may move on more freely. We ask the inner criticized child to accept our gratitude for how well she has done and encourage her to take risks again. We understand. We acknowledge. We tell her it's a new day now. The spirit never left. It may have gone underground for a while but it's back. We are given memories so we can accept our strengths and limitations and move on with healing and new attitude.

"Memory is the diary we all
carry about with us."
—Mary H. Waldrip

Our foundation is found in the past. The richness of today is grounded in many of the same things the child in us loved. To be child*like* is to be soulful. To be childlike is to bring the spirit of innocence and exploration into our days. In your journal, record times when you were childlike and treasure your spontaneous nature.

Many writers, such as Virginia Woolf, felt that the past was the great breeding ground of creativity, a time when the seeds are

"How we remember, what we remember, and why we remember,
form the most personal map of our individuality."
—Christina Baldwin

planted. Those of us writing in our journals today understand this thought. We allow the seeds to bloom or we dig them up to see what

161

"Remorse is the poison of life."

—Charlotte Brontë

their meaning was to be. Just to dig in the fertile soil enriches us. Just to explore. We sort and sift. We decide which memories are to be our companions and which to let go of. When in doubt, I dialogue with my inner child. If she wants me to remember something difficult, I'm glad to be a witness and do this. I also help her remember the special days of paper dolls and scissors.

"A long past vividly remembered is like a heavy garment that clings to your limbs when you would run."

—Mary Antin

I work with many people who have regrets about their lives. I have found that not much good comes from regret. I went looking for a quote for one client who felt terrible about the way she had let down a friend. I found the words of Aldous Huxley helped both of us: "If you have behaved badly, repent, make what amends you can and address yourself to the task of behaving better next time. On no account brood over your wrongdoing. Rolling in the muck is not the best way of getting clean." We live, we learn, we make changes, we move on.

I find great comfort in the idea that the past is the beginning of the future. I think of the past as the dawn. You can walk in the day learning from the dawn and exploring the world in its freshness. As the world becomes lighter, you can see all your joys and sorrows that you walk through. These events belong to you and you can use them to live in a soulful way. You can gain empathy for yourself and spread that to others who need a blessing today.

Exercises

1. List the messages of the past and flip them over. For example, "I am lazy" becomes "I am thoughtful."

2. List the messages of the past and use them. You might remember being called "too active" and now you can say with good self-esteem, "I have good energy. I am active. I am athletic."

3. Write about your changing point of view. You might write about what it meant to be an aesthetic child and how that was put down. Now you can write all the good being an aesthete gives you and others. How it has affected your home, friendships, work in good ways.

4. Choose your right name. How might that reflect you? Throw out clothes and write about it. What does this have to do with your past? Are you throwing any memories out? Your future?

DAY 2: PRESENT TIME

André Gide once said, "It is now, and in this world, that we must live." It is always the right time to do what's right for yourself. To appreciate the soul around you makes the present a delight! You are given feasts of gifts for you to live around. Just now there is a cat at my window and a hummingbird enjoying the nectar of the Mexican sage. The sun is about to set and the wind is still, the end of the day humid. If I can find my spirit to join what is, I love the present.

"The present is the point of power."

—*Kate Green*

Journals are a wonderful place to record your life today. Just remember to share not only events but insights, perceptions, doubts, and wonderings.

"The present is elastic to embrace infinity."

—*Louis Anspacher*

In a proposal for a more humane and livable world, Sulak Sivaraksa of Thailand told a story of the day a religious leader came to visit the Buddha and asked, "When one follows your Way, what does one do in daily life?" The Buddha replied, "One walks, stands, sits, lies down, eats, and drinks." The man asked, "What is so special about that?" And the Buddha answered, "An ordinary person, though walking, standing,

163

lying down, eating, or drinking, does not know that he is walking, standing, lying down, eating, or drinking. When a practitioner of the Way walks, he knows that he is walking. When he stands, he knows that he is standing." This is a classic story of mindfulness.

I try to remember to be mindful in my everyday life. I want to notice how things actually are. I want to notice that I get to be alive. I want to feel the soul in others and laugh with the high spirits of those in the café or on the street. I want to use the world as my playground and let each minute teach me about aliveness. I am trying to live what Saint Paul said. "I have learned in whatsoever state I am in, therewith to be content."

Buddha contemplated his own death to awaken to the joy that is available in the present moment. How could contemplating your death bring you more to this moment? What would it be like to live each day as if it were your last?

Make a writing plan for yourself, set up a writing ritual of when and where and how much time, write out a commitment to yourself and follow it. This is the day you have. Give your spirits what it needs.

"When I don't write, I feel my world shrinking. I feel I am in prison. I feel I lose my fire and my color. It should be a necessity, as the sea needs to heave, and I call it breathing."

—Anaïs Nin

Exercises

1. Read the following ideas and write down an affirmation for yourself to help you stay in present time. For example, "I love the weed that grows through the cracks" can be changed to "I grow where I need to grow. Today is my day for growth."
Try these.
   - Gentleness is a force in life.
   - We all have dark days of fear and doubt.
   - I think of the past and the future and today.
   - I don't want to whine.
   - How can I be helped when there is so much suffering?
   - The present is a mix of the past and future hopes.

2. Do a kind act and write about it.

3. Put on a raincoat and dark glasses and listen in on a conversation just enough to get a sense of what they are saying. Use *streaming* to see what the subject or emotional content mean to your life today. Listen again and write again. Include your intuitive feelings. What are you learning about yourself?

DAY 3: TRANSITIONS

I'm a great wiper. I relax by wiping tabletops and counters. To putter around my office or house is very relaxing for me. I've come to see that it's the way I make transition from one activity into another. I've learned that just a bit of physical energy released like this helps me ready myself for whatever comes next. A walk also helps me transition. Before bed I drink hot milk and read a good novel, inspirational quotations, or some favorite poetry. Reading is a bridge between my day-to-day concerns and the nourishment of sleep and dreaming.

However you transition, it is important that you allow this for yourself. These pauses help you feel yourself and your spirit. Sometimes, in the down time, you'll find the greatest spirituality because it's a time when you can allow habitual routine to become conscious choice where you are alive and noticing.

> *"If what I was watching, evaporated before my eyes, I would remain."*
>
> —Anna Truitt

When you feel stuck think of yourself as in-between two things and name those two things. It will help you realize that you are not really stuck. You are through with work for the day and on your way to relaxation. Next you will decide how to relax, but first why not

"We don't know who discovered water, but we're certain it wasn't a fish."

—John Culkin

listen to soothing music? Or you have left a high-powered job and are wondering what to do next. You are between jobs. You don't have the answer yet. Perhaps you need to add relaxation and research for this in-between place.

In the cycles of life, transition seems to be the most feared and the least understood. Transition is a good time to develop a better sense of spirituality because this time is fraught with uncertainty, and awareness often emerges during uncertain times. There's a saying that life's a casting off. It's true for all of us. We can see the reality of life: birth of something new, development, and change. We see this in ourselves and in mother nature. We need to expect transition to happen and to embrace the lessons of this cycle of life. Transition is a perfect time to have a journal close at hand.

"Often the search proves more profitable than the goal."
—*E. L. Konigsburg*

What I like best about transition (and hate most about it) is that it is a time of life wandering. We don't know what we are doing. Not exactly. Not quite. It takes some trust to be between jobs, between youth and middle age, between relationships and causes. It takes a lot of faith to not be the person you once were and yet not quite the person you are about to be. It's a seesaw and it's a time of unsure footing. This is when a wise teacher can help when we write to her and hear her answer "I am with you. Be patient. Be in balance. Talk to others. Take time for yourself."

"I will have no locked cupboards in my house."
—*Gertrude Bell*

Community can make life's transitions more manageable and even fun. Whatever we share is eased. Perhaps in your journal you can explore finding a support group to use in one of your life's wandering times. It's good to have put something into place when you are on a plateau and things are going well. Many people follow a twelve-step program or a spiritual writing group for this. Make up your mind to let others be close to you when you are unsure.

Often, in times of transition, we review our life. Do not fall into either/or thinking. Your soul holds many qualities of good and bad. Your life has contained good and bad. When you live in a wounded world such as we do, you must understand yourself and your spirit in relationship to systems. You may have had a hard time as a secretary not because you hated the work but because you weren't respected. It didn't have to be a lowly job, but in the system it was women's work and not valued. It helps to write and clarify what you liked and didn't like and what the system poisoned for you. Review your life as lessons and not failures. It's what your earth mother wants for you, learning and grace, not blame.

We can learn from how we characteristically deal with endings. Once you develop a style for endings, you tend to hold on to this feeling even when endings are in your best interest. Endings are a trigger for old memories of shame and fear. I remember a time of losing faith and thinking "I'll deal with this somehow." My style was to clench and to know it was up to me and I was alone.

"There are some things you learn best in calm, and some in storm."
—Willa Cather

Do you initiate endings or do you delay endings? Whether you overstay or leave abruptly, you are reacting to the break in the continuity of things. Neither way is better than the other, but it will help you explore what a good choice for you might be in today's situation. In the exercises we'll explore what your style is and what you may want to keep or let go of.

I have a sense now that life is really a wandering, and part of our spiritual path is to find out how to deal with times of wandering. I have a friend who once in a while says, "Let something new happen." She looks in her mailbox. She believes the fortunes in fortune cookies. She eagerly awaits the phone to ring. She knows, really, she must pay attention to inner signals that something new is coming her way. The shift may be an idea or an external circumstance, but what is important is how she resonates to it.

Clients often tell me that they don't have the time or money to make things happen differently. At the same time, I've seen seemingly impossible things happen. College degrees at sixty. Travel on a shoe-string budget using youth hostels at seventy. Great chances taken by a formerly conforming people. What they have in common is a shift in attitude, when everything lines up and seems to point to a certain action and they believe in it. They set up the next action step by step, and use the route provided in their dreams or from their bodies and inner knowing.

Perhaps writing will help us learn there is a promise in emptiness. How can we give in to emptiness and not try to escape it? How can we write to emptiness? We need emptiness to see our birth and death and rebirth from a new perspective. If we are lucky, we can see ourselves with insight.

Recount in your journal your feelings when you are wandering and don't know where you are going. Times of not knowing can bring information of who you are and what you like. It can show you how you deal with life.

Exercises

1. Use *gazing into the waters* and recall experiences in your life that required an ending. Write the endings in your life down in the best chronological order you can. You might start with ending time at home with mom and beginning school. You might remember the ending of being the only child. Perhaps there was a pet's death or a departure of a parent. The first baby-sitter. The first time you realized you weren't most important. Incidences on a team or at school. Move on to when you first left home and your endings in school, relationships, and jobs. Recall what you felt and what your mind-set was.

2. Write down the answers to these questions: How have I handled endings in the past? What was good or difficult about that style?

How are my feelings the same today? How is this situation different? How am I different? What options do I have? What would be best for me to do if I followed the teachings of my wise voice? What affirmations might I write out for myself and practice?

3. Compare your life to that of your same sex parent. What was your parent doing at your age today? What are the similarities? Go through the transition times of your life and see if there are some corresponding situations and feelings. How are you like and not like this parent? Write about this.

DAY 4: AGING

Age came on tiptoes and left her marks on me. It happened so gradually I didn't notice for a long time. Then one day I discovered I had lines in my lips, which was why my lipstick was caking. I told a friend, "But I don't feel old. I'm somewhere just past the middle of my life and I have half of what I want."

"The birds sing louder when you grow old."
—Rose Chernin

No matter, age was mine to reject or enjoy. I found I liked being with people who hum the same tunes I do but hated realizing I wasn't avant-garde anymore. Then a flash came. When I was young I had this wild idea that the lessons of life were learned in the first half of life and that the second half was for resting and downside. Now I know that is the arrogance of youth speaking. Youth brings experiences in so fast, we often don't take the time to process what has happened, and so we repeat ourselves. Aging takes its time. Without meaning to, I found myself politicized about the aging process and had something new I wanted to write about.

Even if it didn't seem as active or modern, I had the choice to do what I wanted. Staying current isn't as important to me now as it was to the self who wore black nail polish and wrote poems of rebellion and loss. I discovered the truth in what Dorothy L. Sayers writes in *Strong Meat*: "Paradoxical as it may seem, to believe in youth is to look backward; to look forward we must believe in age."

I remember seeing two seniors rushing down a street in Berkeley wanting to get home before it turned cold and before the news. They triggered a memory of how, as a child, I had promised myself I would never go to bed early. I would go to all the plays, all the movies, out every night to hear music. It never occurred to me that there might be joy in easier living, matinees, and reading at night. I was concentrating on feeling alive through connection with the world. It never occurred to me that I would change. Or that I might balance that with connection to myself and my spirit.

In a poem I once wrote, I said, "I sit and think of pine trees and green grass. / My friend dreams peppermint. / Our hormones bounce. We hot flash. / We let our tummies go. We don't care. / We are round like water-smoothed stones. / We use babushkas to cover our heads / from the wind and sing when the silver breezes come. / We smile, We rock. We're together. / We're changing seasons. / We sit on the bench in the sun." And so we did. We also went snorkling off the Isle de Maderas in Mexico and slept on a public beach in Mexico.

"Age seldom arrives smoothly or quickly. It's more often a succession of jerks." —Jean Rhys

Writing need not keep us young. We have had enough days of that. Writing helps us step into the age we are, what we decide it is. Writing becomes our teacher.

You may start with short writing forms such as journal entries and letters and find the fascination with words leads you to creative writing. That's great and it's an interesting craft to learn. What we most care about in all of this is, "Who have you become while writing?"

In *The Measure of My Days*, Florida Scott-Maxwell, a suffragette, writer, and analytical psychologist studying under Carl Jung writes: "We who are old know that age is more than a disability. It is an intense and varied experience, almost beyond our capacity at times, but something to be carried high. If it is a defeat it is also a victory, meaningful for the initiates of time, if not for those who have come less far."

"I am luminous with age."

—Meridel Le Sueur

We have many stages and we are all things. How good it is to listen to spiritual teachers who have lived into middle age or old age. Thich Nhat Hanh is in his sixties. His writings bring us a freedom to explore a way of living that suits our spirit.

"In youth we learn; in age we understand."

—Marie von Ebner-Eschenbech

We can use our writings as our teacher. We can combine the external with the internal and learn through our writing what it is we need to know.

"Perhaps one has to be very old before one learns how to be amused rather than shocked."

—Pearl Buck

Exercises

1. Write down what you felt when you left childhood for the teen years. Young adulthood. When did you feel you reached adulthood and mature adulthood, if you feel you did? What do you see now that you didn't see then? What do you think the future holds in terms of your aging? How can you make it even richer? Discover the secret that sits in the center and knows about aging.

2. Time line your life by age passages that you remember. What is stirred in you as you review these passages? What do you look forward to about aging?

DAY 5: DEATH

How to deal with pain and dying has always been a part of spirituality because it is so inescapably a part of life. The aim is simple: Spirituality helps us live and die well. We face our inevitable dying and death. We want to look at death and suffering calmly and have a conscious death. Facing our dying, we begin to live in love with the day.

By paying attention to endings we practice dying while living. These endings may be in partnerships, friendships, jobs, saying goodbye to one stage of life and greeting a time when school can no longer hold us, a city must be left, a home, or a time of life that was particularly poignant. Since change and endings are one of the constancies of life, we have plenty of opportunity to practice. Our spirit allows us to see what was once only painful as an important part of life, the death of large and small things. I know my worst breakup in a partnership became a great gift, a reminder of who I am and what I want from life. Writing a secret, secret journal of hate and revenge and love and shame helped me through the death of this long-term relationship. I wrote about my dreams in which my lover came to me in a block of ice and I had the ice pick to save or destroy. Explore how you might take another look at an important ending and find new meaning about yourself and your spiritual path.

I recently experienced a tragedy that weakened my belief in my connection to a higher power, challenged my beliefs, and, ultimately, started my belief growing again. My closest friend, Suzanne, committed suicide after suffering for many years from undiagnosed Addison's Disease. She was my wise woman. It was the last thing in the world I expected. She didn't deserve her illness or her life ending that way. No one does.

I learned to handle the grief with less belief, less strength, less hope than I felt I needed. Still, it was enough and I lived. I had to accept once again that life is unplanned, unreasonable. I learned, once again, that I am not in charge. I was thrown back to my spiritual search. Spirituality was something Suzanne and I shared. I lit candles and wrote. I turned for guidance to the statue of the black Madonna she had given me months before her death. I collected rainwater and washed in it. I don't know why.

For many months, I had to be content with questioning and small bits of faith. Suzanne's death created a questioning place in my belief. Why do bad things happen to wonderful people? Where was the goddess? Was she absent or was she holding her? Where do I put my love and belief now? Can I love again? Can I trust her ending? If she was my wise person here on earth and she took her life when the suffering was unbearable, can I call that a bad thing? How can I hold all of this? I learned that a questioning belief is still a belief and that deep belief can hold questions, doubts, certainties, and blessings.

"I have been in sorrow's kitchen and licked out the pots. Then I have stood on the peaky mountain wrapped in rainbows, with a harp and a sword in my hand."

—Zora Neale Hurston

I learned the hard way that a shaken strong belief can grow again. Perhaps with more hesitation and questioning, but this time there is something in our human spirit that calls us home to ourselves. I try to remember that her ending was not her life, and that her life held much joy. I pray that she is at home in peace.

After Suzanne's death I wrote poems about wanting to bring bushels of green grasses to her, of placing a stick in the ground as a marker so I would not forget my grieving or her pain when others were sick of my talking about this. I wrote about her entering my dreams, and how I could be a presence for her in return. I wrote about her as my apple tree, still giving shade and apples, just giving out at the bark.

"All sorrows can be borne if you put them into a story or tell a story about them."

—Isak Dinesen

We can journal our pain about a loved one's death and ask ourselves: How have we been blessed by our lives and this person? What will we have to strengthen in ourselves now? We can ask if our loved one has met themselves and what they might better know now. We can ask if we have met ourselves.

My sister called me to break the news when my father died. I told her to tell me slowly what was wrong. I asked her to repeat herself. She had the grace to do as I asked. For a while I didn't tell anyone that my father had died. I didn't want to take care of them. I didn't know how to take care of myself just then.

I wrote. Writing was a way to get totally focused, totally submerged. It heightened the awareness of his death. Sometimes it gave me a break. It helped me reframe the experience from despair and shock to peace and acceptance. It gave me a chance to write out my mixed feelings about him and our relationship.

I found a support group that was centered on writing feelings about loss in a pictorial journal. We wrote about photographs we had of and with our loved ones. We found pictures that reminded us of our relationship. I found a picture of a circus and wrote and wrote. It acknowledged the man who gave me a ride on his shoulders to the neighborhood carnival when I was just four years old. I learned to incorporate pictures in my own journal by using them as writing inspiration.

Finally, I could feel myself settling down a bit, and I sensed that my father's spirit had become calmer, too. Or was this the same? This peace came after much support and much writing. Feelings had been released from my body. I could imagine he was fishing in a beautiful spot far away from the city lights under which he lived all his life. He had loved the quiet and the beauty of mountain lakes. Now he didn't fall in, get tangled in lines, just caught huge bass. I couldn't save him. However, I could love him even in death.

Most people die as they live. Live a spiritual life and call upon these beliefs at death for yourself and your loved one. Have a mantra to use in distress and use it at death. Alice, a client, remembers a passage from the Bible from her childhood and although she has left formal religion behind she finds it natural to use it as her mantra: "Yea, though I walk through the valley of the shadow of death, I shall fear no evil: for Thou art with me." She's a woman of gratitude and courage and I expect that legacy will shine through the dying journal she is keeping for her children.

We must be willing to give up our ideas of death and dying, at the end, and enter into the movement of death as it is.

"Death, when it approaches, ought not to take us by surprise. It should be part of the expectancy of life. Without an ever present sense of death, life is insipid. You might as well live on the whites of eggs."

—Muriel Spark

Oscar Wilde once wrote: "The final mystery is oneself. When one has weighed the sun in the balance, and measured the steps of the moon, and mapped out the seven heavens star by star, there still remains oneself. Who can calculate the orbit of the soul?" We need to learn our limits. If depression comes, we must remember that even when we feel as if nothing will get better, change is sure to come. We look at a pond and the water is calm. Beneath, the water is teaming with life. So it is with us. We need not despair. The spirit works in miraculous ways.

There are many ways to practice dying when we are on a spiritual journey. We write about the experience of our death. To die while we are alive will free us to treat this physical world without attachment, for we will see that we own nothing. We can awake to what we really have, which is ourselves and this day. We can trade our watch for a compass.

Exercises

1. Write down five "big" questions, then use *clustering* and *streaming* to explore them. You might start with "Why am I here?"

2. What worries you about death? Give attention to your feelings and let them engulf you. Then spill those feelings all over the page. Write about death as the stranger you want to know.

3. We don't know how we will die or when, or what survives. What are your thoughts on these issues? Do some wild writing with large paper and crayon and see what "shadow thoughts" are brought up and scrawled across the page. Let your thoughts rip! Now take any surprising thoughts to *gazing into the waters* and *streaming*.

4. If this were the last day of your life, what would you do? What if this were the last year? How would you rearrange your priorities? Write out new commitments you can make to yourself. Use *listmaking*.

DAY 6: REBIRTH

There are many ways to imagine rebirth. Some of us have felt reborn after a period of depression. Cavernous days lighten and we find ourselves gradually enjoying the sunshine and the world's activity around us. Finally, we realize we enjoy music again and notice we are reborn. We have the reminder of the past imprinted in us and the lessons thereof. However, we have moved on with more grace.

After any loss we can ask ourselves what still lives? Who am I now? You can list what you are grateful for today. You can explore in writing who you will be. Sometimes, after loss, we become more independent and learn to reach out better. We have to dig deeper into the bedrock of ourselves and find a steady place. Writing may deliver us to our new self.

A client told me of a child who died in his sleep at ten. The doctors found no illness, no physical reason for his death. He was a healthy, happy and a hands-on child. He was an immediate, outgoing person. After his death, his mother had a dream in which she was given the message that he was given this life as a short one. She believed in the power and clarity of the dream. It felt to her that her son had lived as he was supposed to and it was up to her to grieve his absence and accept this. He was in a place of rest between lives just now.

A friend received a color pastel drawing of her daughter as she died in a car crash. A local artist who has seen angels all her life read an article about the child's death and sent the picture of her body rising to heaven with wings and grace. Her arms were stretched upward with heavenly intent. My friend found this comforting whenever she thought of her daughter's death. The angel woman has angels hanging in the United Nations and has used her visions to comfort people all over the world. She says she can feel the release of energy as someone dies and they go to rebirth.

A client from Viet Nam was afraid of the ghost of her sister. We explored in writing what she believed in that was different from her parents and culture and realized she actually believed in a loving spirit that could be her guide. My friend, Luca, believes in more than spiritual presence and energy. He believes the gods watch us and want to live in a physical body. When we die, they choose us and live in the physical realm to work out our unfinished lessons. Luca publishes journals and helps readers work out their issues. He wants to return.

Do you believe in an afterlife? Do you believe in reincarnation or the migrating soul? Whatever you believe, believe in grace, that you will be cared for.

Another way to think about rebirth is to watch the plant world. I love annual flowers. But perennials remind me that much beauty and good happens around me without my effort—how the lavender, early sunrise, blue fountains, delphinium, dianthus, Mexican sage, fuschia bless my garden every year. I love the flying saucer coreopsis and the fan flower. These plants show me that life returns.

"The power that makes grass grow, fruit ripen, and guides the birds in flight is in us all."

—Anzia Yezierska

Writing's importance is not in what you produce but in who you become while writing. Hopefully, you will feel many twinges of rebirth until the day comes when your beliefs of regeneration and eternal life are clearer to you.

Japanese director Kore-eda Hirokazu directed a fanciful tale about memory, mortality, and the sting of regret. In the movie, called *After Life*, twenty-two people, young and old, have just died and are being held at the way station between earth (life) and heaven. They are each asked to choose a memory to take as a companion into the next life. Videos of their life are available and they can see reruns of any memory to make sure this is what they want to choose. The way station and the calm behavior of the "newly dead" is interesting to watch as they tell of their life and death. It is interesting to watch the process of choosing or not choosing a memory. The staff who help the transitioning people haven't chosen a memory yet themselves. By helping others decide, they often come to a decision for themselves. The "newly dead," or the "transitioning people," seem focused and content in carrying out their task of choosing a memory. They easily talk about their death and how it happened as if it were in the past and resolved.

Who knows about past lives? When I was first doing hypnotherapy, Marla, a singer with the Chicago opera, came to me to work out interpersonal issues. She had been told she was too assertive. She was a large, blond-haired woman with incredible energy and life force and talent. When she regressed to childhood through hypnotherapy, she reported being in a small Belgium town. She recognized the church from a postcard she once received. She had never been there but had resonated to the picture of that church. And she was always curious about Belgium.

This regression wasn't her childhood in Detroit. She seemed to be describing a past life. She was a young man who was mute. She saw her struggle as balancing her life of "large voice" with the previous life of "no voice." In the former life, she had learned to communicate in other ways and was more in touch with nuances of behavior and was more likable in some ways. "Balance," she told me, " balance again, but at least I can forgive myself and see why I go to such extremes."

It no longer mattered whether I believed in past lives. Some clients were going to go into a past life and it could be helpful. I decided it was not my business to believe or not believe, but to lead my clients to the place where their life could be healed. Metaphor or past life, it gives comfort and promotes growth.

Marla wrote a wonderful story about the boy she once was and said it was the first time she sat and wrote in many, many years. She came several times each season, and the last time I saw her she had started a past-life journal.

It's up to us to remember that "the world is round and the place which may seem like an end may also be only the beginning," writes Ivy Baker Priest, the former United States treasurer. I didn't know how wonderful life could be until I lived through a century of life's cycles. Each year of life becomes precious. Writing will help you realize this as you use your journal to connect to your spirit.

"Life can't defeat a writer who is in love with writing, for life is a writer's lover until death."

—*Edna Ferber*

Exercises

1. What do you believe today about life and rebirth? Use *streaming* to explore how those concepts have changed, if they have, over the years. Do you believe you will change to new beliefs? What might they be?

2. What is sacred ground for you in terms of life, death, and rebirth? Do the *Peace Meditation* (see appendix, pg. 184) and then write.

3. What memory would you take into the afterlife? Use *gazing into the waters* and then *streaming* and write down a past life you might have had. You can believe in it or write it as a story. How could this memory or story help you?

4. The apple is grown in orchards that, in Celtic law, were specially protected as sacred groves on holy ground. Celtic tree-lore describes their uses both on the physical and magical level. The otherworldly land of Avalon, to which King Arthur was taken after his last battle, means "the place of apples." Write about your experiences with apples and apple orchards and explore how you might use the apple as part of your spiritual writing and ritual.

DAY 7: REWARDING YOURSELF— THE GRAND ADVENTURE

For your reward this final week, think about a place you have been wanting to go for a long time. It can be a neighboring city's rose garden, a small town not so far away, or an island in the great Pacific. You can go to the attic where you once wrote and set up a writing area again. Wherever it is, give into an urge you've been neglecting. Plan to go there. Go there. Take your journal and write what permits or

"Far away there in the sunshine are my highest aspirations. I may not reach them, but I can look up and see their beauty, believe in them and try to follow where they lead."

—*Louisa May Alcott*

doesn't permit you to have what you want right now. Write down what the world of your wealth is today. Write down how the state of your birth, the feeling of your future, and the wanderings of today affect and show who you are. Write what you know about rebirth in living. Write what your soulful self wants you to know.

APPENDIX:
THE TECHNIQUES REVISITED

I thought it would be helpful to put all the techniques together again here as a handy reference. This way you can refer back to the techniques whenever you need a refresher. They really are a marvelous way of entering a writing mind.

Streaming

Just start writing across the page. Keep going. Write your name if you don't know what else to write. Continue without much thinking. Don't stop. Make doodles to fill in the lines if you have nothing to say. Pay no attention to the inner critic. This is your time to wonder. This is a time to be curious and explore. After several minutes of being "present" with your writing, you'll find you're in a shift. You've really let go and are just writing. Keep going. After you've written for fifteen minutes or more, go back and underline insights and anything you'd like to continue at another time.

Gazing into the Waters

1. Take several deep breaths into your "belly." Pay attention to your breathing, in and out.

2. Focus attention on the top of your head and slowly shift your awareness down your body until you reach your toes.

3. Imagine yourself descending a stairway while counting from one to ten. Feel your body going down, stepping slowly.

4. Imagine yourself arriving at an entryway and moving through it into a place you find calming, perhaps a quiet garden or sandy seashore. What surrounds you? Where do you sit? What do you see? Use your senses to sharpen this special place: sounds, fragrances, feelings, body sensations, something to touch, something that beckons. This is a place to use over and over until just remembering it calms you. From this place, you can explore whatever you like.

Dialoguing

Write down the names of ten teachers in your life. The teachers may be actual classroom teachers, neighbors, parents, or influential adults from whom you have learned valuable lessons. A teacher may also be a quality such as time or patience. Be sure to have one of your ten teachers be your own wise speaking voice, the self you are developing spiritually through your writing.

Now, write down a concern. Maybe you're wondering if you should stay in a relationship even though you have greatly changed through the years and would not choose this person if you met today. It could be a concern about not liking to be alone and wondering how you could learn not to feel so empty.

Look over your list of teachers and see which teacher could help you out with this particular concern. Imagine a conversation with this teacher.

Clustering

Begin by choosing a word you want to write about. Write it in the center of the page, then write down every word that comes to mind. Write down words even if they don't make sense. Write down words that seem odd or silly. You can work in a circular fashion. Keep

concentrating on doing this and you'll feel a shift in your consciousness as words just occur to you. Write them down quickly before the
judge censors them.

Notice how one word leads to another. Sometimes, your mind will
jump to a more concrete word or an unexpected one. Do the clustering in whatever way works for you and you'll seed your fertile soil. You
can start with the word *inspiration* and see where it takes you. Later,
you can do some *streaming* from the ideas or feelings that emerge from
the cluster. You can take a "wing" of the cluster and do some *streaming*
on that section and see what new insights arise.

Listmake

Listmake organizes your thoughts and can be used as a jumpstart for
streaming. Listmake by writing a list of what you like about yourself.

Make a list of the feelings you'd have to give up if you lived as though you really liked these things about yourself. Now use *streaming* and imagine yourself in a conversation where you really liked yourself.

Peace Meditation

The Peace Meditation helps us feel our feelings rather than watching what our mind does. Those feelings are connected to our self-knowledge. This meditation leans on the pause and lets us keep in touch with our body and its breath but gives us room to feel.

1. Notice the *out breath*. Say "old" as you breathe out. This releases you from the past.

2. Now notice the *in breath*. This gives you time to pause between out breaths; it gives you time to feel your feelings. The in breath is an opening. It helps you practice patience. Notice how expanded you feel.

Dream Sourcing

1. Write down a dream.
2. Choose the main feelings in the dream.
3. Choose the main images.
4. Decide in a sentence or two what the dream is about.
5. Give the dream a title.
6. Decide the question the dream asks.
7. Do wise speaking dialogues with the main images/people of the dream.
8. Ask each image/person for a gift.
9. Tell the meaning of the dream. Or reverse the meaning of the dream.

Coming Together

1. Write down your dream.
2. List the main players in the dream. They could be a neighbor, a cat, an ice cream cone, a friend, your sister or brother.
3. List the actions of the main players. For instance, the neighbor retreating from a cat's hissing, a cat hissing.
4. Write down how each of the main players is a part of you.
5. Acknowledge all parts of yourself and, using *gazing into the waters*, ask the dream what it wants you to know. You may want to then ask how your parts can work in harmony since they are all a part of you. You might, for example, decide the part of you that is afraid must learn from the hissing part how to defend you.

ABOUT THE AUTHOR

Janell Moon's childhood diaries were filled with her adventures in nature's arms and the wonder of Ohio's rivers and green hills. Heaven drifted through her braided hair and she used writing, then as now, to help her understand herself and her spirit through the changing seasons of her life.

Moon is a writing instructor at the College of Marin and at San Francisco Community College. She has a private practice as a counselor and hypnotherapist in San Francisco. She has spent twenty years helping people to better understand themselves and find their spiritual and creative voice. She uses writing as an important tool for the journey toward wholeness.

Her fourth book of poetry, *The Mouth of Home*, was recently published by Arctos Press and is distributed by Baker & Taylor & Small Press Distribution in Berkeley, California.

For information on individual sessions or workshops, Moon can be reached at janellmoon@aol.com.

RECOMMENDED READING

Bender, Sue. *Everyday Sacred: A Woman's Journey Home.* San Francisco: HarperSanFrancisco, 1996. Tales of the sacred in every day.

Bethards, Betty. *Dream Symbols.* Boston: Element Books, 1997. Interpretation of dream images.

Bolles, Richard. *The Three Boxes of Life.* Berkeley: Ten Speed Press, 1976. Action for life/work planning.

Cameron-Bandler, Leslie, and Michael Lebeau. *The Emotional Hostage.* San Rafael, Calif.: FuturePace, 1986. How to use your emotions wisely.

Claxton, Guy. *Hare Brain, Tortoise Mind.* Hopwell, N.J.: Ecco Press, 1999. Appeals to readers to be less analytical and let creativity have free rein.

Daniels, Rosemary. *The Woman Who Spilled Words All Over Herself.* Boston: Faber and Faber, 1997. Ideas on how to teach writing.

Dillard, Annie. *The Writing Life.* New York: Harper Perennial, 1989. Her experiences as a writer.

Edgarian, Carol, and Tom Jenks. *The Writer's Life.* New York: Vintage Books, 1997. Quotes from famous writers.

Epel, Naomi. *The Observation Deck*. San Francisco: Chronicle Books, 1998. Ideas on personal writing.

Goleman, Daniel. *Emotional Intelligence*. New York: Bantam Books, 1995. How to use your emotions to help make sense of the world.

hooks, bell. *Remembered Rapture*. New York: Henry Holt and Co., 1999. The writer at work.

Knight, Brenda. *Women of the Beat Generation*. Berkeley: Conari Press, 1996. Women who broke with convention to forge American literary history.

Kopp, Shelton B. *If You Meet the Buddha on the Road, Kill Him!* New York: Bantam Books, 1972. You must believe in your own inner-teacher voice.

L'Engle, Madeleine. *Glimpses of Grace*. San Francisco: HarperCollinsSan Francisco, 1995. Help in forgiving.

Maxwell, Florida Scott. *The Measure of My Days*. New York: Viking Penguin, 1969. Finding contentment.

Peirce, Penney. *The Intuitive Way*. Hillsboro, Oreg.: Beyond Words Publishing, 1997. A guide to living from inner wisdom.

Ragan, Kathleen. *Fearless Girls, Wise Women & Beloved Sisters: Heroines in Folktales from Around the World*. New York: W. W. Norton & Company Ltd., 1998. International stories of female heroines.

Rico, Gabriele Lusser. *Writing the Natural Way*. Boston: Houghton Mifflin Company, 1983. Using right-brain techniques to release your expressive powers.

Seaward, Brian Luke, Ph.D. *Stressed Is Desserts Spelled Backward*. Berkeley: Conari Press, 1999. Tips for less stress.

Sher, Barbara. *Wishcraft.* New York: Ballantine Books, 1979. How to get what you really want.

Stanek, Lou Willett. *Writing Your Life.* New York: Avon Books, 1996. Putting your past on paper.

Vanzant, Iyanla. *Acts of Faith.* New York: Fireside, 1993. Daily meditations for people of color.

West, Celeste. *Words in Our Pockets: The Feminist Writers Guild Handbook* San Francisco: Booklegger Press, 1986. A very useful guide to feminist publishing.

Wolf, Naomi. *Promiscuities.* New York: Random House, 1997. Rethinking women's sexual being.